THE COURT OF
BETTER FICTION

DEBRA KOMAR

THE COURT OF BETTER FICTION

Three Trials, Two Executions,
and Arctic Sovereignty

DUNDURN
TORONTO

Cover image: Courtesy of MEARS Online Auctions
Printer: Webcom, a division of Marquis Book Printing Inc.

Title: The court of better fiction : three trials, two executions, and Arctic sovereignty / Debra Komar.
Names: Komar, Debra, 1965- author.
Description: Includes bibliographical references and index.
Identifiers: Canadiana (print) 20189065605 | Canadiana (ebook) 20189065613 | ISBN 9781459744080 (softcover) | ISBN 9781459744097 (PDF) | ISBN 9781459744103 (EPUB)
Subjects: LCSH: Tatamigana, -1924 | LCSH: Alikomiak, -1924 | LCSH: Murder—Nunavut. | LCSH: Trials (Murder)—Yukon. | LCSH: Inuit—Canada—Government relations. | LCSH: Inuit—Legal status, laws, etc.—Canada. | LCSH: Canada—Ethnic relations.
Classification: LCC HV6535.C32 N9 2019 | DDC 364.152/3097195—dc23

1 2 3 4 5   23   22   21   20   19

We acknowledge the support of the **Canada Council for the Arts**, which last year invested $153 million to bring the arts to Canadians throughout the country, and the **Ontario Arts Council** for our publishing program. We also acknowledge the financial support of the **Government of Ontario**, through the **Ontario Book Publishing Tax Credit**, **Ontario Creates**, and the **Government of Canada**.

Nous remercions le **Conseil des arts du Canada** de son soutien. L'an dernier, le Conseil a investi 153 millions de dollars pour mettre de l'art dans la vie des Canadiennes et des Canadiens de tout le pays.

Care has been taken to trace the ownership of copyright material used in this book. The author and the publisher welcome any information enabling them to rectify any references or credits in subsequent editions.

— *J. Kirk Howard, President*

The publisher is not responsible for websites or their content unless they are owned by the publisher.

Printed and bound in Canada.

VISIT US AT

 dundurn.com | 🐦 @dundurnpress | ⨍ dundurnpress | 📷 dundurnpress

Dundurn
3 Church Street, Suite 500
Toronto, Ontario, Canada
M5E 1M2

In memory of RCMP Corporal Jim Galloway, killed in the line of duty February 28, 2004 — one of the good guys.

Loved ones demand honesty, but what they really want is better fiction.

— David Byrne, *The New Sins*

Contents

III: TRIAL BY ERROR

IV: RECKLESS PROPHECY

Map of Canada's northern coast, including Nunavut and the Northwest and Yukon Territories. Although the relevant place names remain the same, in 1921 Nunavut and the Northwest Territories were combined. The distance between Tree River, NWT, and Herschel Island, YT, is approximately 692 miles.

Prologue

On December 6, 1921, Royal Canadian Mounted Police Corporal William Doak arrested a young Inuit male named Alikomiak a few miles inland from the northeast coast of the Northwest Territories. Alikomiak was accused of murdering his uncle, the final blow in a series of retaliatory killings between rival families. He did not resist arrest and went willingly with the RCMP officer to the Tree River detachment.

The police outpost had no holding cell, forcing Doak to detain Alikomiak in the barrack's storage shed. Doak was not a large man, but he towered over the prisoner, who was "quite young, short and [of] very slight build."[1] Alikomiak's cringing obedience soon earned Doak's trust and he was given free run of the small detachment, performing menial tasks to appease his captor.

As the first feeble signs of spring arrived in 1922, Doak's subordinates were all otherwise engaged, leaving him alone to supervise the accused.[2] On March 31, Doak threw his sealskin long boots at a sleeping Alikomiak, then pointed to their fraying soles. He mimed a stitching motion, an implicit order to repair the boots. When the Inuit captive finished resoling the first boot, he showed it to Doak. The enraged corporal threw the boot back at Alikomiak. "I had not done it right," Alikomiak later said, adding, "I was mad and did not feel good inside."[3]

The next morning, Doak used the rare moments of privacy to sleep in. His service revolver was within easy reach, holstered and draped over the bedpost near his head. Just before sunrise, Alikomiak went into the "unlocked Police store house" and took a rifle and four bullets. He crept into the barracks and saw "that Doak was still asleep ... on his right side with his face to the wall." Alikomiak moved to the left of the cook stove ten feet from Doak's bed. He raised his rifle and fired once, hitting Doak in the left buttock.

The corporal awoke with a scream. He tried to sit up, but was in too much pain. Rising onto his left elbow, Doak looked at Alikomiak and shouted, "What is the matter with you?"

Alikomiak bolted out the door, but he paused to look through the window near the wounded man's bunk. He saw that "Doak had turned in his bed with his legs hanging over the side and his head against the wall. He was groaning and his eyes were sometimes open." Blood flowed from the corporal's mouth and Alikomiak knew "he was close to dead."

The Inuk returned to the sleeping quarters. He lifted Doak's legs onto the bed and covered him with a blanket. Doak eventually lost consciousness and was dead before the sun cleared the horizon. According to police, Corporal William Doak would not be the only man Alikomiak killed that day.

He was arrested later that afternoon by Constable Daniel Harrison Woolams at a seal camp seven miles from the Tree River detachment. He did not resist arrest, asking only to change his boots before surrendering to police.

Alikomiak made a full confession through an RCMP translator. In his statement he recounted the killing in graphic detail, including Doak's final words. That confession would be the sole evidence against Alikomiak in the trial that followed.

There are several glaring inconsistencies in Alikomiak's account, irregularities that investigators, the prosecutor, jurors, and the judge failed to notice at the time and that all legal scholars studying the case have failed to notice in the decades since. One of the most obvious was that only two people were in the room when Doak was killed: the victim and the perpetrator. Alikomiak could not speak a word of English and Doak knew nothing of the local language.[4] Throughout his incarceration the two had communicated exclusively through hand gestures. So, how could Alikomiak possibly have known what Doak said in the moments before he died?

I: DIFFERENT SCALES

During the past 10 years there have been 7 white men murdered by Eskimos.... In addition there are known 17 murders among the Eskimos themselves, not including the victims of infanticide.

In all, there are not more than 3000 Eskimos in the Canadian Arctic, and a record of 24 known murders in such a sparsely peopled country indicates that the native is not as mild and gentle as described by some.

In the same period there is no record of the killing of a native by a white man.

— *Mail and Empire*, October 23, 1923

One

Pristine Wasteland

In all ways that matter, the European invasion of the Arctic began when the English explorers Martin Frobisher and Henry Hudson sailed into the bays destined to bear their names. Little heed was paid to the Indigenous residents who had already named those bodies of water. This willful indifference established the template for Canada's policy regarding the Far North. Land mattered more than the people on it and, like a toddler with an oft-abandoned toy, Canada only cared about the Arctic when someone else wanted it.

That interest came in waves driven by the winds of commerce. European explorers like Frobisher and Hudson rode the first wave, heading northward in their quest for the elusive Northwest Passage and its promised trade route with the East. The second wave brought whalers from Norway and Britain. Accustomed to bitter climes, the whalers ruthlessly harvested the waters, leaving the rotting carcasses of more than eight thousand whales in their wake.[1]

The foreign whalers occasionally made landfall, turning far-flung outposts such as Herschel Island, with its plentiful supplies of liquor and local women, into sites of "unprecedented debauchery." During brief moments of sobriety, the whalers noted the region's natural resources and returned home with tales of untapped riches.

Natural resources of a different sort spurred the third wave as the Hudson's Bay Company began lapping at the Arctic's shores. In 1670 King Charles II had granted the Honourable Company exclusive trading rights to all lands draining into Hudson Bay, a region dubbed Rupert's Land. The company initially focused its efforts on the bountiful southern shores of the bay, leaving the frozen North to its Indigenous inhabitants.

Rival trading companies from the United States were only too happy to plunder the neglected northern shore, and while those in Ottawa expressed little concern, the steady American encroachment sparked fears in Britain. Under growing pressure from London, the HBC transferred control of Rupert's Land to the Dominion of Canada in 1870. Ten years later, when the United States again tried to extend their jurisdiction into the Far North, England issued an order-in-council ceding the Arctic Islands to Canada, effectively saving the fledgling nation from its own negligence.

Canada's continued reluctance to assert its authority over the North sent a tacit signal that the Arctic was "open territory." In 1874 the United States and Norway began squabbling over mineral rights on Baffin Island, dismissing Canada's tepid claims to the region. Those working the foreign fishing boats plying the Hudson Strait also thumbed their noses at Ottawa's murmured objections.

Even then, Canada was slow to anger or action. More than two decades of unchecked foreign pilfering would pass before Minister of Fisheries Louis Henry Davies dispatched Dr. William Wakeham to Baffin Island with strict orders to do ... something. In a ceremony short of pomp, circumstance, or attendees, Wakeham formally proclaimed Canada's sovereignty over the Arctic on August 17, 1897.

Wakeham's declaration failed to have the desired effect, forcing Parliament to again stake Canada's claim by drafting the Northwest Territories Act of 1905. While the act clarified some domestic issues, it did little to shift global perceptions of Arctic sovereignty.

When proclamations and legislation proved futile, Canada had little choice but to put boots on the ground. In 1913 the government funded the Canadian Arctic Expedition. Led by Vilhjalmur Stefansson, the mission was given five years' funding and a loose mandate of scientific and geographic exploration. It was understood Stefansson would plant the Canadian flag on any land he "discovered."

In order to plant that flag, Stefansson soon learned he would first have to push the Arctic's Indigenous residents out of the way. In all ways that matter, it was the first time any official Canadian representative acknowledged the Inuit.

Two

The Mounties and "These People"

An excess of snow and the absence of colour wreaks havoc on the mind. Time distorts, unmoored by seasons or circadian rhythms. Sound bounces effortlessly in the frigid air, travelling distances that are impossible to judge even with well-trained senses.

Vilhjalmur Stefansson was no stranger to such environments, having helmed prior explorations in Alaska and Victoria Island, but his dispatches from the Canadian Arctic Expedition reveal a man equally awed and confounded by everything, and everyone, he encountered.

Stefansson's accounts detailed the mechanics of Inuit domestic life. Distance was clearly an enemy. The daily struggle for basic necessities — food, heating fuel, shelter — forced the sparse Indigenous population into isolation. Small bands, often no more than a dozen families, carved out fragile existences by separating themselves from competing camps. Catchment areas encompassed long stretches of barren landscape, harvested to the point of depletion before necessity or a shift in the weather compelled the band to move on.

Such isolation fostered change. Languages splintered into myriad local dialects — some intelligible to neighbouring bands, others not. Trade suffered, as did marriage between bands. Rivalries flared and often turned violent. Bands foraged for themselves and, for the most part, kept to themselves.

Stefansson's reportage of the Indigenous people had a decidedly more scientific bent than Adolphus Greely's tales of "Blonde Eskimos" published one year prior in the *National Geographic* magazine, but the nation's newspapers, and their readers, embraced Greely's colourfully skewed vision of the Inuit. Indeed, the true nature of life in the Arctic was lost on those blessed with seasonality and resources. White perceptions of the Inuit centred on the myth of a "monolithic" North in which all Indigenous people were a single band of "Eskimos."[1] Beliefs as to the character of this monolithic band broke down into two schools, with 60° north latitude serving as the clear dividing line.

Those south of 60° saw the Inuit as harmless curiosities, a sentiment reinforced with the release of *Nanook of the North: A Story of Life and Love in the Actual Arctic* in July 1922. The seventy-nine-minute silent film was an instant box office sensation. Shot in northern Quebec by Robert J. Flaherty, a prospector for the Canadian Pacific Railway, the documentary staged hunting scenes in which Flaherty replaced the locals' rifles with spears.[2] His exotic depictions were the perfect visuals to complement the rose-tinted tales of Jack London.

Residents north of the sixtieth parallel held a far less romanticized view. Scattered reports of Inuit violence soon prompted calls for organized law enforcement. The North-West Mounted Police, the forerunner of the RCMP, was modelled after the Royal Irish Constabulary. Initially a vaguely paramilitary organization staffed by former soldiers with little to no police experience, the NWMP first established posts in the Yukon to maintain order during the Klondike Gold Rush. In 1900, the force's authority spread north of the Arctic Circle when the first permanent Arctic police post was established in Fort McPherson in 1903.[3]

Newly posted Mounties in the region believed "an orgy of slaughter was sweeping the igloos." Police reports described the Inuit as "lawless," and willing to "slit your throat for a box of cartridges."[4] This perception, coupled with ubiquitous misinformation regarding the Inuit practice of infanticide, had justified the force's recent "legal imperialism" of the Arctic.[5]

Such imperialism bore the stamp of governmental approval. Ottawa "has all of its contacts with the Eskimo through the Mounted Police," explorer Knud Rasmussen noted.[6] While Rasmussen admired the Mounties' willingness to be all things to all people, he feared they could not "justly be expected to substitute for all of the agencies of civilization."

With the weight of a nation's unrealistic expectations on their shoulders, the Mounties moved progressively northward, determined to bring law and order to a land and a people with their own sense of justice.

........————————————........

In 1920, Corporal William Andrew Doak was infected with the poetic view of the North spread by Jack London's *Call of the Wild*.[7] When the RCMP asked for volunteers to man their latest, most northern outpost in the Territories, Doak raised his hand. At age thirty-eight, he was already a fifteen-year veteran of the force. A confirmed bachelor, Doak had spent two years as a bugler in the military before joining the North-West Mounted Police on June 3, 1905.[8] He became a Royal Canadian, trading his black serge for red, when the force changed its name on February 1, 1920.[9] His only regret in his new posting was that he was now a Mountie without a horse.

At first a life of regimented service seemed a poor fit for William Doak. He was reprimanded three times in his first tour — once for neglect of duty and twice for being "very much under the influence of liquor" — earning him a total of twenty-seven dollars in fines and two punitive ten-mile hikes.[10] Doak swapped vices during his second tour, trading alcohol for tobacco in all its forms,[11] and soon embraced a life of discipline. His service over the next twelve years was "exemplary."

When asked what the police were, the region's Inuit replied "the rich men of the country."[12] Compared to the Inuit he served, Corporal Doak was indeed well off. His posting as commander of the Tree River detachment earned him a monthly salary of seventy-five dollars, plus four walls and a roof which he shared with his three subordinates and their Inuit translator.[13]

The five men slept in a sixteen-by-eighteen-foot room with a rudimentary kitchen and not much else.[14] Bathing and laundry were done in a small tub of water heated on the coal-burning stove. For everything else, there was an outhouse crafted of snow and ice. The detachment's small pantry was stocked with dry goods from the Hudson's Bay Company outpost conveniently located two hundred yards to the north, across the ice of a small bay.[15] As they rang in the New Year of 1921, Doak, his three

A family portrait of William Andrew Doak, circa 1920. Born on August 4, 1883, Bill was the sixth of nine children. He was raised Methodist by his Irish-born father, William, and New Brunswick–born mother, Margaret.

constables, and the three HBC traders were the only "white men" in the entire region.[16]

The Tree River detachment was established in 1919 to stave off Russian and Scandinavian interest in the Coppermine-Coronation Gulf region. A secondary mandate was to "prevent murders of whites" by the Indigenous population, opening the Arctic for commercial and governmental activity.[17] "Native-on-native" crime was a growing concern in the region, although treated far less seriously than "native-on-white" violence. Desperate to demonstrate Canadian sovereignty, the Mounties gave little time to cultivating relations with the Inuit and had little interest in learning the customs and language of the local people. Order was maintained through force rather than co-operation. In their rush northward, the RCMP also neglected to install one crucial element in Tree River: a holding cell to detain prisoners.

Men willing to endure the hardships of the North were hard to come by, but the brass at RCMP headquarters believed Doak was the perfect candidate to police the Arctic. Well-liked by his colleagues, Doak was "described by all as a decent man,"[18] a "general favourite" who was "always willing and cheerful under the most trying conditions."[19] Better still, he was not above "assuming a brutal and terrifying manner" to keep the local populace in check.

Bluster was all he had. Doak was a blond, blue-eyed slip of a man, standing barely five foot six and tipping the scales at a mere 140 pounds. His thirty-five-inch chest did not inspire fear, although his tattooed forearms lent him a faint air of menace.[20] Doak's bombast was largely for show, a manifestation of his belief that his Inuit constituents were "primitive and violent" with each other but "docile" under the controlling hand of white authority.[21] That belief, and the lack of a holding cell, would be Doak's undoing.

Three

A Christian Crime

The Inuit neither needed nor wanted the Mounties and their one-sided quest for justice. They had their own well established notions of jurisprudence, an unwritten yet fixed set of traditional laws for dealing with those who stepped outside of societal norms. Shortly after Corporal Doak arrived, these duelling legal systems collided.

It all began with a "shooting affray,"[1] the RCMP's toothless euphemism for a massacre that left five Inuit dead. Throughout 1920 and into the following year, Alikomiak's band mates took up arms against each other in an escalating series of sexual transgressions, insults, and overt acts of aggression that left their camp tense and fidgety.

In the spring of 1921, Alikomiak's uncle Pugnana was living with the band in their seasonal camp on the mainland south of Kent Peninsula, along the northern coast of the Northwest Territories (now Nunavut). Pugnana had earned a reputation as "one of the toughest men of the tribe" by being "very quick with gun and knife."[2] He had been caught stealing from caches and was no longer welcome in the community.[3] Pugnana refused to leave.

Mates were scarce in the insular society, and competition among males was fierce. Another member of the band, Ikialgagina, made sexual advances toward Pugnana's wife, Agnahiak. She refused him, but the slight was not forgotten.[4] In a neighbouring snow house, Pugnana's nephew Tatamigana

Tatamigana, circa 1923.

was having an affair with the wife of Hannak, although Tatamigana claimed Hannak approved of the arrangement.[5] After months of backbiting, imbro-glios, and threats, Hannak and Ikialgagina entered Tatamigana's igloo and sat on either side of him, intent on murder.[6] A last-minute intervention by another band member saved Tatamigana, but the matter was far from settled.

In hindsight, no one could pinpoint the exact moment the violence erupted one morning in June 1921. Seemingly without provocation, Hannak became violent, shouldering his rifle and wounding Anaigriak.[7] Pugnana responded in kind, and soon everyone had their weapons drawn. Throughout the mêlée, Tatamigana had his uncle Pugnana's back.[8]

It ended as quickly as it began, with five lying dead: Ikputuwak, Ikialgagina, Hannak, his wife (also named Pugnana), and their four-year-old daughter, Okolitana.[9] Her chances of survival without parents were virtually nil, and the RCMP later called the child's death "an act of mercy."[10]

The carnage did not satisfy Pugnana. In the days that followed, he began carrying a loaded rifle at all times, telling his camp mates "he did not care what happened to him."[11] He asked Tatamigana to help him again, but his nephew refused, later stating, "I did not want to kill any more as I had had enough."

Pugnana taunted Tatamigana for his cowardice, saying his nephew was "no good and did not know how to shoot."[12] Tatamigana bore the insults in silence but kept a nervous eye on his increasingly unstable uncle.

Traditional Inuit law held that those who kill without remorse must be killed to protect the band. Retaliation was an accepted, albeit rarely necessary, method of maintaining harmony in such tight-knit communities. The band council recognized that Pugnana's downward spiral warranted action, and it fell to his family to carry out the will of the leaders. Modern Inuit legal scholars, such as Aupilaarjuk, contend that what Tatamigana did next was justified.[13]

In September — "about the time the snow was first coming" — Tatamigana went fishing with Pugnana at a creek one day's journey from their summer camp.[14] His cousin Alikomiak accompanied them.[15] When Pugnana was out of earshot, Alikomiak told Tatamigana of the plan to kill their uncle as payback for the June rampage. Tatamigana agreed, telling Alikomiak he would kill Pugnana if Alikomiak did not because Pugnana had said he "was no good." As a show of faith, Tatamigana handed Alikomiak a brand-new shell for his rifle, then loaded another into his own gun.

Alikomiak, photographed at Fort Good Hope in the summer of 1923. In a statement to police, Alikomiak claimed he had traded ten white arctic foxes for a rifle at the Hudson's Bay Company outpost on Kent Peninsula one year prior.

Their plan was simple: Tatamigana would "make signs" with his eyes when the time was right to fire the fatal shot. Alikomiak would shoot Pugnana from behind so he would not see it coming. According to Aupilaariuk et al., shooting the victim unawares is in keeping with Inuit traditions of retaliatory justice: "They never let the murderer know that he was going to be killed. He was never told this in advance."[16]

The next afternoon, Pugnana asked his nephews to go hunting for squirrels.[17] The three set off at midday, shouldering their rifles as they headed into the woods. Pugnana blazed the trail, followed by Alikomiak as Tatamigana lagged behind. Pugnana carried his rifle over his left arm, his right hand loosely covering the trigger. Tatamigana slowed his pace to catch Alikomiak's attention. As the two fell back, Tatamigana gave Alikomiak the signal. Alikomiak raised his rifle and fired, hitting Pugnana squarely between the shoulders. As Tatamigana later told police: "The bullet came out through his chest. Pugnana fell on his face and did not speak. He died quickly."

The co-conspirators then "moved the body a little way and covered it with earth so that other people would not find it."[18] To calm the roiling tensions in the band, they agreed to tell no one what they had done. When they returned to camp the next day, they told the others Pugnana had gone hunting.

No one challenged their story, and no one mourned Pugnana's death. Several band members quietly went in search of the body and the clandestine grave was soon discovered. Before the winter freeze, Pugnana's siblings gave him a proper burial.

News of the June massacre eventually reached Corporal Doak at Tree River, located more than one hundred miles and "three to four days travel" from the summer camp.[19] In August 1921, RCMP Inspector Stuart T. Wood — normally stationed at Herschel Island off the Yukon coast — was making his annual rounds when he learned of the "shooting affray" from an Indigenous fur trader. When he reached Tree River, Inspector Wood instructed Corporal Doak to investigate as soon as weather permitted.[20] Wood left standing orders to bring the perpetrators to Herschel Island for detention and trial.

On December 3, 1921, the weather finally cleared.

Four

Worlds Collide

The Tree River detachment had no boat, deemed a luxury item in a region with mere weeks of open water each year. All patrols were restricted to dog-sled during the winter months.[1] On December 3, Corporal Doak — recognized as "the best traveller and dog driver in the district"— began the onerous journey to Kent Peninsula to investigate the massacre. Accompanying him were Constable Woolams and their translator, Cyril Uingnek.[2]

Four of the band's ten families had fled the summer camp in the wake of Pugnana's killing spree. Doak needed several days to locate the surviving witnesses, but he eventually interviewed Anaigriak (who was wounded in the fray) and Agnahiak.[3] The RCMP team then travelled an additional two days to locate Tatamigana at a separate encampment and place him under arrest. In his initial statement to police, Tatamigana identified Alikomiak as Pugnana's killer.

Alikomiak had gone inland to rejoin his parents in the months since Pugnana's murder. Corporal Doak set off in search of the trigger man, leaving Woolams to guard Tatamigana. After three days of hard sledding, Doak finally found Alikomiak. The Inuk surrendered without a fight, although his band mates were not so accommodating.[4] As Doak later noted, "the natives of this village were not particularly friendly, for according to their customs the boy had just done the right thing in killing Pugnana." Doak

Corporal William Doak (on the right) with Gerald Chisigalooh on winter patrol along the Mackenzie River, circa 1916. The men were en route from Herschel Island to Fort McPherson.

strapped Alikomiak to the dogsled and beat a hasty retreat before more blood was spilled.

Doak and Alikomiak returned to the summer camp to reunite with Woolams and Tatamigana before setting off for the detachment. "While on his return journey to Tree River," an RCMP report later noted, "yet another murder, which had taken place in the fall of 1921, was brought to Corporal Doak's attention by another band of Eskimos."[5] An Inuit man named Ikalukpiak had killed his partner Havoogack in a fit of jealous rage. After a brief investigation, Doak took Ikalukpiak into custody.

Alikomiak suffered frostbite in both feet while mushing back to Tree River. Doak chided Alikomiak for "not being married" and having "no one to make his clothes and boots." The patrol was forced to shelter at the Hudson's Bay outpost on Kent Peninsula until December 24 when the prisoner was again fit to travel.[6] On Christmas Day the police party and their prisoners returned to the barracks at Tree River.

No formal charges were laid, nor were there any indictments. According to a report by the RCMP assistant commissioner, the plan was to wait for the spring thaw "when navigation opened up" to "transfer the three murderers, together with the witnesses, to Herschel Island, where the Police Headquarters for the District are located. It was at this point that the preliminary hearing of the cases was to be held."[7]

In the meantime, detaining the prisoners at a detachment with no holding cell proved difficult. Doak gave Alikomiak "little hard punches" to keep him in line, but Tatamigana was not so easily controlled.[8] Doak wanted to separate Alikomiak from his band mates, and he assigned Constable Woolams and Cyril the translator to escort Tatamigana, Ikalukpiak, and the key witnesses to the seal camp seven miles from the Tree River Detachment. An HBC trader named C.H. Clarke agreed to accompany Woolams and help guard the prisoners whenever he was not out checking his trap lines.

Doak typed his formal report with the force's customary brevity, but he shared his true feelings about the Kent Peninsula patrol with a passing HBC trader named Philip Godsell. Doak told Godsell the massacre was "just another family mix-up … same old story. Some Huskie got too handy with his knife, the rest piled in."[9] Doak also lamented he now had "to bring the whole caboodle back to Herschel Island."

Despite his little punches and tough talk, Doak was not entirely without compassion. Alikomiak's frostbite had left him hobbled and in great pain. Pitying his charge, the corporal kept Alikomiak in Tree River "for treatment," setting in motion the chain of events that would ultimately lead to his own death.[10]

Days before he was killed, Doak told Godsell: "I've expected trouble … the Huskies seem to think all they've got to do if they want a good time at the white man's expense is to put a snow-knife or a bullet into someone. First thing you know, it won't be safe for any white man in Coronation Gulf."

Five

The Threat of the Mundane

As Alikomiak watched the life drain from Corporal Doak's body on April 1, 1922, one of Tree River's other resident white men was pulling on his boots. Hudson's Bay Company trader Otto Binder was a creature of habit. He rose every morning with the sun, ate a hearty breakfast, then crossed the frozen bay at eight o'clock to visit with his friend William Doak. That morning was no exception.[1]

Doak may have followed a literary call of the wild to the Far North, but Binder had heeded a more mercenary siren's song. In his early twenties, Binder briefly tried his hand as a hunter in Nome, Alaska, before heading east in search of bigger game and fortune. In 1916 he boarded the schooner *Challenge* and was "left behind" to set up a hunting camp on the southeast shore of Banks Island.[2] One year later, Binder travelled to Kellet, where he met Vilhjalmur Stefansson, who was by then half-way through his Canadian Arctic Expedition. Stefansson mistook the German-born Binder for an American, in part because Otto had his "eyes on fur and a fortune."[3] Stefansson admired the young man's ambition.

The following year, Binder and two colleagues purchased the *Challenge* from Stefansson. Binder wanted to sail the ship to Coronation Gulf, where he planned to buy fur from the Inuit. The dream died when the schooner ran aground off the coast of Amundsen Gulf.[4] Binder eventually made it to

Otto Binder and his fellow crew members offload the cargo from the schooner *Mary Sachs* near Kellet in 1917. Binder had previously scavenged the ship with the permission of her captain at the time, a man named Gonzales.

the Copper River, where he signed on with the Honourable Company as a trader and clerk in 1918.

The job suited Binder, who had a "very quiet and kindly disposition."[5] His superiors believed he was "well liked both by the natives and white men," although local traders begged to differ.

On that April morning, as he made his way toward the RCMP barracks, forty-one-year-old Binder had been in the service of the Hudson's Bay Company for less than four years, every minute spent in the two tiny wooden buildings that made up the Tree River outpost. Binder's once-peripatetic lifestyle had come at a cost, and he was tired of being lonely. To ease that loneliness, he had recently taken an Indigenous wife, named Toktogan.[6] The couple had one son and were caring for another boy from her previous marriage.

Binder first met Toktogan at her father's home on Victoria Island, shortly after he began trading fur. The two men struck up a friendship and Binder's attention was soon drawn to the Inuk's attractive daughter.[7] Toktogan's father "offered the girl" to Binder, who "hesitated at first, being a white man and a Hudson's Bay Company employee, but was finally persuaded by the father to take the girl."[8] They married *à la façon du pays* in 1920.

Not everyone celebrated their union.[9] At the time, Toktogan was already married to a hunter named Ikialgagina.

Company politics and tribal intrigue were the last things on Binder's mind, however, as he trudged his way across the frozen surface of the inlet. "The sun was high"[10] and the first cracks of the spring break-up echoed like gun shots in the arctic air. Binder stuck to his well-worn trail, bundled against the cold in his sealskin parka and boots. He had dressed with care but left the house unarmed, carrying neither his company-issued rifle nor his personal handgun, a Savage .32 he purchased from the HBC.[11] It was his lone break from habit, and it would cost him dearly.

Alikomiak's account of what happened to Binder that morning was later accepted by police without question, and that account has passed unchallenged through the hands of social and legal scholars ever since. Modern forensic scrutiny, however, indicates that considerable skepticism was warranted. Still, Alikomiak's oft-repeated version of events, drawn from his police interrogation, provides a baseline from which to begin.

During that interrogation, Alikomiak claimed he knew Binder's habits and was keeping close watch from inside the RCMP sleeping quarters. He ran to the pantry window facing the company store and spotted the trader heading for the detachment. Alikomiak panicked, later stating: "I was afraid that Binder would see Doak and want to kill me."[12]

The Inuk grabbed a handful of shells — "about 10" — and monitored Binder's approach through the window.[13] When Binder reached the half-way point, Corporal Doak issued a final groan. Alikomiak heard the death rattle from inside the pantry and ran into the main room as Doak breathed his last.

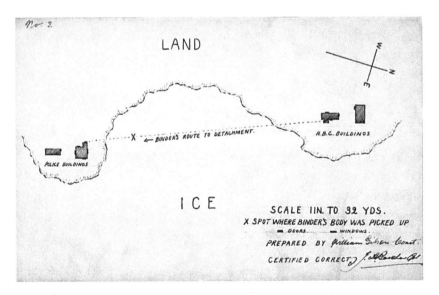

Schematic of the RCMP detachment and the HBC outpost at Tree River. The hand-drawn map was appended to the initial crime report, and marked the spot where Binder was fatally shot.

Alikomiak took hold of a wooden chair, dragging it from the main room to the pantry window.[14] Stepping onto the seat, Alikomiak surveyed the frozen bay. Binder was now only fifty yards away. The Inuk raised his rifle to the top window pane, "aiming to hit him in the head." He pulled the trigger. Binder dropped to the ice, "groaning out loud." Alikomiak later recalled: "The bullet penetrated the lower part of Mr. Binder's heart."[15] The HBC trader "moved a little and was dead quick."

Alikomiak jumped from the chair and ran to where Binder had fallen. He found the trader laying on his right side. Placing his hand on the man's chest, he felt nothing.

Alikomiak ran across the ice toward the Hudson's Bay Company post. Toktogan "had been standing in the porch of the house and heard the shot." She looked across the bay and saw Binder lying on the ice. According to Alikomiak, she began "crying plenty."

"Don't cry anymore," Alikomiak pleaded, "I can't help it. I was scared. I killed both of them."[16] Binder's body was more than Alikomiak and Toktogan could lift, so they dragged him across the ice and into the barracks.[17] "He was too heavy to put alongside of Doak," Alikomiak later stated, "so we left him on the floor" beside Constable Stevenson's bed.[18]

Toktogan then asked Alikomiak to take her home to her people at the seal camp seven miles to the east, and he agreed. She went to the HBC post to dress her two children and pack her belongings. Alikomiak remained in the barracks.

Just then two men from the seal camp — Ayalegak and Toletuk — arrived at the outpost to trade some furs. When they asked to see Binder, Toktogan wordlessly directed them toward the RCMP barracks across the bay. The fur traders found Alikomiak sitting on a bed with his rifle beside him. Staring blankly, Alikomiak whispered: "I have killed the two white men." As a token measure of respect, Toletuk and Ayalegak moved Binder's body onto Stevenson's bed and covered him with an HBC point blanket.[19]

Although neither Ayalegak or Toletuk believed Alikomiak had done anything wrong — at least according to Inuit law — the men warned him his actions were "too bad," and there would be hell to pay from the police.[20]

It was a good story, simply told, and never doubted. The physical evidence of the scene, however, recorded another tale.

Six

A Cursory Investigation

When Binder's wife returned to the barracks, Ayalegak and Toletuk bundled the woman and her two sons onto their dog team's sledge. Exhausted and overburdened, the dogs strained through the deep snow toward the seal camp. Alikomiak, running behind the sledge, had little trouble keeping pace. While en route, Alikomiak reportedly told his travelling companions there were still a few white men left in the region. To avoid any reprisal, Alikomiak announced his plan to kill two of them — Constable Woolams and HBC trader Clarke — once he reached the seal camp.[1] Fearing further bloodshed, Toktogan convinced Alikomiak to unload the shells from his gun before they arrived at the village.

Once in camp, Toletuk asked Alikomiak to give up his rifle and he handed it over without protest.[2] Ayalegak and Toletuk then "rushed in" to Constable Woolams's snow house. As each man shouted to be heard, they told the officer, "Alikomiak had done the killing of these two white men."[3]

Woolams ordered Cyril Uingnek to fetch Alikomiak from Toletuk's igloo. When Cyril returned with the suspect in tow, Alikomiak was placed under arrest. Woolams then asked Clarke to ready his dog team. At 3:15 p.m., with the sun already low on the horizon, Woolams, Clarke, and Alikomiak returned to the Tree River detachment, arriving just after five o'clock.[4]

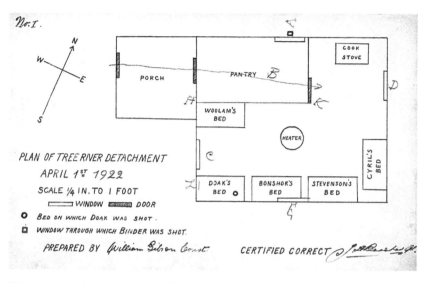

Diagram showing the interior of the RCMP barracks at Tree River. The map was prepared as part of Constable Bonshor's initial investigative report.

The RCMP barracks was freezing cold. The fire in the coal stove had died hours before, and arctic air rushed through the bullet hole in the pantry window. "After lighting the lamps," Woolams placed Alikomiak in irons.

The constable found Doak laying on his back with his head toward the foot of the bed. Laying a hand on his fallen commander, Woolams noticed "his body was still warm." Clarke examined the wound, noting "the bullet had entered a little below the small of the back and to one side and apparently had pierced up through the bowels or lungs as his mouth was full of blood." There was no exit wound.

Binder's final moments were captured in the scene. Bloody drag marks led from the barrack's door to the place where the trader had fallen dead. The chair Alikomiak had used to reach the window stood as a silent reminder. Woolams also noted the "window facing the HBC post was broken, and it was through this that Binder had been shot." Alikomiak filled in the blanks using a series of hand gestures, pointing to the chair and pantomiming the rifle's discharge.

Clarke found Binder lying on Stevenson's bed, covered with a blanket. He had a through-and-through wound and had "died instantly." As Alikomiak looked on, the two men wrapped the bodies in additional blankets, then carried them into the storage shed.

With night falling, Woolams, Clarke, and a manacled Alikomiak made the long trek back to the seal camp. Once there, Alikomiak was unshackled and detained in one of the camp's snow houses. The only thing keeping him there was his fear of the white men, their guns, and the miles of frozen wasteland stretching out in every direction.

In the wake of Doak's death, Woolams assumed temporary command of the detachment. When fellow constables Bonshor and Stevenson returned from their mail run, Woolams decided they would heed Inspector Wood's standing orders: the prisoners and witnesses would be sent to Herschel Island for processing. A subsequent inventory revealed the detachment lacked the dogs and feed necessary to make the journey. Woolams felt transferring Alikomiak was the priority; the others would follow by schooner when the weather turned and the HBC supply ship made its annual call.

Three weeks later, Constable Stevenson tied Alikomiak to a dogsled. Peter Norberg, the manager of the Kent Peninsula HBC outpost, accompanied them on the 692-mile odyssey west toward Herschel Island. The group broke their journey at Fort McPherson before travelling the final 125 miles aboard the *Shamrock*, a schooner owned by a local Inuk.[5]

While at Fort McPherson, Alikomiak enjoyed the same freedom he had at Tree River.[6] Inspector Wood's wife, a frequent visitor to the fort, saw little reason to fear, saying: "The Eskimos were cheerful, helpful and to all appearances harmless, and I was accustomed to dispensing with the ordinary safeguards of civilization."[7]

Stevenson told the Fort McPherson officer, Constable Myhill, of the murders of Doak and Binder — it was the first time anyone outside of Tree River had heard the horrific tale. Myhill in turn carried the news to the RCMP headquarters in Edmonton.[8] On July 20, 1922, Major G.L. Jennings telegraphed the information to the assistant RCMP commissioner in Ottawa.[9]

The first media accounts of the story appeared the next morning, although many of the facts — including the victims' names and the location of the crimes — were misreported.[10] By far the worst offender was the *Calgary Herald*'s July 22 report entitled "Eskimo Bad Man Kills Two Whites at Herschel Post," which identified the victims as Constable Boak of Herschel detachment and G. Binder of the HBC. The *Herald*'s factually challenged account served as the basis for many subsequent accounts in smaller regional papers. Another racially charged account suggested the killings were a hate crime carried out by a deranged Inuk who "hated the Whites."[11]

As the outside world learned of the tragic events in Tree River, Stevenson and his charge continued their journey. They arrived at Aklavik, the only major detachment on the mainland near Herschel Island, in the fall of 1922. Alikomiak was placed in the detachment's holding cell, where he spent the winter waiting to see what came next.

Seven

One Time Too Many

Good judgment is derived from experience, and experience is born of poor judgment — a sentiment epitomized by the Canadian legal system at the turn of the twentieth century. Trial-by-error was the norm in a country whose courtrooms were simultaneously straining to break free from and yet embrace the model of an oppressive British progenitor. The dissonance was loudest when it came to First Nations issues. At that time, Canadian law was cut-and-pasted from British Common Law. England had no Indigenous population and, as a consequence, Canada had nothing on the books to address its Indigenous population in the wake of Confederation. The result was a piecemeal abomination of bench law — derived from precedent rather than legislation — in which any judge's decision became the nation's governing principle.

In 1876, Parliament introduced the Indian Act, an amalgam of existing precedents and statutes pertaining to the Indigenous Peoples. (The first significant amendments to the act would not come until 1951. Additional amendments were made in 1985.) The act had limited scope, however, as it pertained only to the southern First Nations; the Métis, Inuit, and northern Indigenous populations were not covered by the bill.[1] Bench law alone would determine Alikomiak's fate and, as he surrendered to a system ill-equipped to deal with him, the only relevant precedent was a masterclass in mixed signals, paternalistic imperialism, and flawed reasoning.

--------------- ——— ---------------

In 1913 two Oblate priests — Jean Baptiste Rouvière, thirty, and Guillaume Le Roux, twenty-six — travelled north to the Coppermine River with a loose mandate to convert the Indigenous people. It was a task for which they were wholly unsuited. Neither man spoke or understood any of the Inuit dialects, nor did they possess any demonstrable survival skills or experience in harsh winter conditions.[2]

The ill-prepared missionaries soon found themselves lost in a snowstorm, stranded with nothing more than their dog team and a growing sense of panic. Two Inuit, Sinnisiak and Uluksuk, had followed the priests' tracks through the snow and overtaken them just in time. The priests offered to give them animal traps if the locals guided them back to safety. The Inuit agreed but, after a few hours of hard-sledding, Sinnisiak and Uluksuk changed their minds and declared their intention to return to their camp.

A desperate Le Roux threatened them with his rifle, and the Inuit pretended to fall back in line. Moments later, Sinnisiak pulled his snow knife, crept up behind Le Roux, and stabbed him in the back. Uluksuk took his own blade and finished the job. As Rouvière tried to run, Sinnisiak shouldered his rifle and dropped him with a single shot. The Inuit then set upon him with a knife and an axe.

Sinnisiak used his knife to slice each priest open from his throat to his navel. He then rummaged through the viscera until he found each man's liver. He slivered off two pieces from each organ, taking one for himself and offering the other to Uluksuk. The Inuit ate the offal raw, a ritual to prevent the dead men from coming back to life. The Inuit left the gutted remains and claimed the dogsled, weapons, and the promised animal traps before heading back to their camp.

The RCMP did not learn of the murders for more than a year, and they did not arrest Sinnisiak and Uluksuk until 1916. The two Inuit first stood trial in Edmonton one year later, charged only with the murder of Rouvière.

Public sentiment favoured the accused. Those south of sixty largely ignored the tales of cannibalism and postmortem mutilations, reasoning instead that the priests "had disturbed the primitive innocence of the Inuit and had got what they deserved."[3] The accused's court-appointed lawyers argued self-defence, and the jury agreed, acquitting both men.

Neither the RCMP nor the Department of Justice was prepared to let the case drop. A few months later, a second trial was held in Calgary, this time on murder charges stemming from the death of Le Roux. Self-defence was raised again at trial — a far more fitting defence, given that Le Roux had threatened the Inuit with his rifle — but the Calgary jury was not swayed.

Sinnisiak and Uluksuk were sentenced to life imprisonment and sent to the RCMP detachment at Fort Resolution to serve their time. With no long-term facilities to hold the men, police had little choice but to release them in 1919. The RCMP commissioner and the justice minister rubber-stamped their release, believing the two killers had "a role to play in educating the Inuit in the ways and power of Canadian law."[4]

With their wrists gently slapped, Sinnisiak and Uluksuk returned to their families, laden with the trade goods they had acquired during their stay at Fort Resolution. While incarcerated, the two had learned a smattering of English and were quickly hired by the RCMP detachment in Tree River as guides and dog handlers. The two convicted men were still on the payroll the day Doak and Binder were shot dead.

The Government of Canada had shown leniency in the hope that a firm warning was sufficient to bring the Inuit in line and curb future "native-on-white" violence. Canada trusted the message was clear: British justice applied to the northern First Nations, but it could be fair and merciful. Unfortunately, the message received was that crime was a shortcut to trade goods and gainful employment.

Following the deaths of Binder and Doak, the police were no longer in a forgiving mood. Assistant RCMP Commissioner Cortlandt Starnes wrote to Duncan C. Scott, the deputy superintendent of Indian Affairs. Starnes reminded Scott of the Oblate priest killings, calling it a time when "frenzy, superstition, and Christianity were all hopelessly mixed and lead to murder." Starnes now saw the premature release of Sinnisiak and Uluksuk as a curse that seemed "to show that a little Christianity, without someone to guide and direct [it], is most dangerous for these people."[5]

Starnes would not allow history to repeat itself. "Kind and generous treatment of the natives who have committed murders in the past has apparently had the opposite effect to that intended," wrote Starnes, "and I am afraid there is a danger of the natives concluding that crime is a thing to be rewarded by the white man. In my opinion, steps must be taken to endeavour to impress upon the Eskimo that disregard for human life will not be tolerated and those found guilty of committing murder will be adequately punished."[6]

When word of the latest murders reached Parliament, Prime Minister Robert Borden instructed the police "to quietly bring these people under the influence of the law."[7] Sound advice, but in the end, there would be nothing quiet about it.

Eight
Lucien and Herschel

If the debacle surrounding the murders of the Oblate priests had taught the police or the Department of Justice anything, it was that southern juries were too lenient and enthralled by the Inuit to inflict serious penalties. Furthermore, those entrusted with creating and administering the law felt that the trials had been too far removed from the communities in which the crimes occurred. If the goal was to teach the Inuit of the majesty and power of Canadian justice, shouting that message from the lower half of Alberta had proven a wasted effort.

The Justice Department decided Alikomiak, Tatamigana, and a handful of other accused Inuit would not be brought south for trial; this time, the court would come to the Inuit. It would be the first court held north of the Arctic Circle, a prospect that both thrilled and soothed the halls of power in Ottawa. The swashbuckling age of colonization through exploration and flag-planting was now past. Establishing sovereignty over the North and its Indigenous population had become a mundane artifact of occupation and governmental administration. A sensational murder trial, and its accompanying headlines, was precisely what Canada needed to finalize its claim on the Arctic.

It would not be cheap, nor would it be easy. The government rationalized the expense by saying that "high-profile circuit trials" presided over by non-resident magistrates would "impress the natives."[1] There was also a small band of ministers who naively believed that "justice could be administered without regard to cost."[2] Best of all, the Department of Justice expected a northern jury to be "less sympathetic" to the Inuit,[3] all but guaranteeing the desired outcome.

No one in the Justice Department paused to consider whether the Inuit had their own laws or system of justice, for such a notion was simply inconceivable. Even if the government were to concede that Indigenous law existed, it was easily ignored because it was neither "static" nor written down.[4]

The only question was where to hold the trial. Justice being done was all well and good, but *seeing* justice done became the prime objective. The right visuals were paramount, both for the Inuit and for the press who would carry news of the proceedings back to the civilized world.

Several locations were nominated but quickly dismissed. The list was eventually culled to two prospects: Aklavik and Herschel Island. Both had buildings large enough to serve as temporary courthouses and holding cells for detaining the prisoners.[5] Each also offered reasonable access in the summer — a must if the trial was to attract journalists.

Inspector Stuart Wood, the Herschel Island commander, campaigned hard to have his detachment play host to the trial. Unlike Aklavik, the

The summer settlement on Herschel Island, circa 1925. The Canadian government never dispatched census takers to the island, so the size and demographics of its population were unknown.

island offered "suitable accommodation and enough supplies to feed all the people … without putting the detachment's winter supplies in jeopardy."[6] As a final carrot, Wood assured the Justice Department "there will be sufficient white men" to form "a good jury."[7] Aklavik could make no such claim. The accused would not have a jury of their peers — an Indigenous juror would not be seated in Canada until 1947[8] — but at least there would be enough warm white bodies in Herschel to fill the jury box.

A show trial demanded a suitable backdrop, and Herschel Island looked the part, replete with Indigenous inhabitants in traditional costumes and starkly rugged landscapes. The island was and remains a place of brutal beauty, a speck of wind-swept rock and snow anchored three miles off the Yukon's northern coast. Ice-locked for more than eight months every year, Herschel experiences two intense months of sun, open water, and relative warmth each summer. Any images transmitted to a curious public down south would reveal an alien world of whale bladder water tanks, nomadic tent camps, and stoic-faced people garbed in seal skins.

With the trial's location set, Wood's preparations began in earnest. His superiors in Ottawa leaked the location to the press, ensuring the decision received front-page coverage.

In the days that followed, the Department of Justice was inundated with letters from prominent lawyers and judges offering their services for the historic assignment.[9] A handful were from legal scholars drawn to the case by the constitutional issues at play. The vast majority were from headline hunters and weekend adventurers looking to see the Great White North on the government's dime. Although many applicants argued politics should play no role in the selection of the judicial team, Deputy Justice Minister E.L. Newcombe acknowledged "there is always some patronage about these matters."[10]

The next pressing need was to appoint a presiding judge. Despite the flood of jurists vying for the role, the Justice Department restricted its short list to sitting circuit justices. After lengthy deliberations, Stipendiary Magistrate Lucien Dubuc was selected. Dubuc had bested his competitors because he was the only justice with previous experience holding court in the North. In 1921 Dubuc had presided over the murder trial of Albert LeBeau. Dubuc convened his court at Fort Providence, situated on the mouth of the Mackenzie River 186 miles southwest of Yellowknife. LeBeau was Dene, a

The temporary courtroom at Fort Providence, NWT, during the murder trial of Albert LeBeau, June 29, 1921. Judge Lucien Dubuc presided from an elevated dais in front of the Union Jack.

member of the Slave Nation, and was accused of killing his wife. He was found guilty and later hanged at Fort Smith.[11]

Dubuc's handling of the LeBeau trial had "evoked no criticism," but there was considerable hand-wringing over the "very great expense of his judicial retinue."[12] To save costs, and as a measure of how simple and brief the government believed the trials would be, E.L. Newcombe decided "the judge should be able to report these proceedings without a stenographer."[13] If Dubuc could not contain his retinue, the deputy minister would do it for him.

Profligacy aside, Dubuc was a solid choice to head the judicial party. His career in law was a given as his father, Joseph, was chief justice of the Manitoba Court of Queen's Bench. Lucien Dubuc possessed "the bearing of a French nobleman," with the wardrobe to match, presiding over his court and his life with a quiet dignity.[14] He developed a "healthy disrespect for written law," preferring to create his own precedents, and was a firm believer that the facts of a case were whatever he declared them to be.[15]

Judge Dubuc received his formal appointment to oversee the *King v Alikomiak* and *Tatamigana* on May 11, 1923. Despite the initial penny-pinching by the Justice Department, Dubuc's contract was respectful and even a touch extravagant. In addition to his standard salary (mandated by statute), Dubuc would have all travel expenses and meals covered for him, and a ten-dollar-per-day "allowance" to cover incidentals.[16]

Dubuc's appointment came just in time. The travel window to Herschel Island was small and approaching fast. As he signed his contract, the judge had less than four weeks to prepare to hold court where no court had ever been before.

Five days later, another key role was filled when Irving Brass Howatt was appointed as Crown prosecutor.[17] Howatt seemed a logical choice given

Portrait of Justice Lucien Dubuc. Born on November 29, 1877, in St. Boniface, Manitoba.

his lengthy and impressive resumé. The veteran King's Counsel was born on Prince Edward Island in 1875. After graduating from Dalhousie University, he studied law under A.A. McLean in Charlottetown and was called to the bar in 1907. He joined the prominent firm of Emery, Newell, Bolton and Ford in Edmonton, where he remained for more than a decade.

After a brief tour of duty in the First World War, Howatt returned to Canada to serve as acting attorney general of Alberta for two years.[18] In 1921 he hung a private shingle as Howatt and Howatt, joining forces with his brother Bruce.

His credentials raised no eyebrows, but his health was a cause for concern. At forty-six years of age, Howatt had grown doughy of face and waist, and he had been discharged from the military because he was sightless in one eye. Physical failings aside, Howatt possessed a keen legal mind and all the right social connections. He was a proud Master Mason, a staunch Methodist, and a vocal Liberal, who lived his life by a simple creed: "The harder the conflict, the greater the triumph."[19]

As Howatt pondered the terms of his contract, a far more controversial choice received an offer to serve as defence counsel for Alikomiak and Tatamigana, although the accused themselves had no say in the matter. The deputy minister of justice wanted someone already on the government's payroll.[20] Newcombe's choice — Thomas Lewis Cory — was a solicitor for the Northwest Territories and Yukon branch of the Department of the Interior.[21]

Thomas Cory's growth had been permanently stunted from living life in his father's shadow. William Wallace Cory, deputy minister of the interior from 1905 through 1931, was an astute political animal who accumulated power and titles through guile and ruthless efficiency. Thomas, on the other hand, peaked as a mid-level bureaucrat toiling in the bowels of one of his father's many agencies.

There was little family resemblance. William Cory was whippet-thin, stern, and distinguished, his angular face softened only by a prominent jet-black moustache.[22] Thomas was dumpy and unrefined. If he harboured any of his father's ambition, he kept it well concealed.

Still, any talk of nepotism in Thomas's appointment as defence counsel was misguided. Shortly before Thomas got the nod, his father wrote a confidential letter to E.L. Newcombe strongly recommending another man for the job.[23] Cory did not believe his son capable of handling such a complex case, and Newcombe shared many of his reservations. Despite the doubts expressed by both men, it seems that Thomas had something working in his favour.

On September 12, 1922, weeks after the outside world first learned of the murders of Doak and Binder, Thomas Cory had drafted a memo to his boss O.S. Finnie, director of the northwest territorial division of the Department of the Interior. Cory wanted to call attention to a matter of some concern: "The numerous murders committed by Eskimos in the last year or so clearly indicate that kindness and clemency have not had the desired effect upon the native population." Cory proposed a simple solution: "A court ought to be sent into the N.W.T. in 1923 to try those accused of murder. The cases should be tried midst the accused's local surroundings where the Native will feel the influence of the law."

Cory was certain such a judicial exercise would send a very clear message, adding, "As kindness has failed in the past I strongly recommend that the law should take its course and those Eskimos found guilty of murder should be hanged in a place where the natives will see and recognize the outcome of taking another's life."[24]

Seven months later, Thomas Cory was appointed as sole defence counsel for Alikomiak and Tatamigana.

By contract, both Howatt and Cory would receive twenty-five dollars per day in salary plus per diem and travel expenses.[25] The police reports and case narrative had not yet been sent south, so Newcombe attached several newspaper clippings to Howatt's letter of offer to acquaint the prosecutor with "the facts" of the case.[26] Cory, for the defence, received no such primer.

The final members of the judicial party appointed were the police escorts assigned to provide security and guard the prisoners. Optics alone ruled their selection. "These are all very smart and clean men," wrote RCMP Commander W.R. Lindsay, "and as the scene of the trial will be crowded with Eskimos, they will be very representative of the Force and should create a good impression."[27] Inspector Wood already had enough men on Herschel Island, but Lindsay took a belt-and-suspenders approach: "While I do not anticipate trouble in any way, it must be remembered that the Eskimos are all armed, and their customs are different from ours, and the records of their wars with the Indians show that they are not wanting in courage." It was, Lindsay reasoned, "better to be safe than sorry."

---------———————————————···

II: PRETRIAL MOTIONS

---------———————————————···

The killing of these two white men now makes it necessary for the Hudson's Bay Company to look into matters and bring some pressure to bear whereby an example be made of some of these people.

The natives killed and the witnesses taken by the Police have cost the Company approximately five hundred (500) foxes this winter.... The natives are taking the white man as a joke — "Shoot a white man and live good and have every comfort" — is beginning to be their slogan. Instead of punishment a premium is being given in the fact that they ... have first-class food, see the white man's country, get petted and shown around as a curiosity and then return to their own people much exalted and persons of influence in their own community.

The Police have been established three years and to date the natives have but a vague idea as to what they are being stationed here for, as is shown by the fact that they speak of all native prisoners taken by the R.C.M.P. as "employees" or "the people who are working for the Police."

P.S. — I don't see why damages could not be counted on from the Canadian Government on account of Tree River Post for about $75,000.00. Binder was shot through the carelessness of letting a self-confessed murderer run loose with all freedom.

— C.H. Clarke, HBC trader
Letter to HBC district manager, April 15, 1922

Nine

Impediments

Security was not the only challenge facing the Herschel Island court. There was also the small matter of geography. Canadian law did not permit crimes committed in the Northwest Territories to be tried in any arbitrary location. In its headlong rush to create a show trial, Ottawa added a new layer to the mythos of the monolithic North: the belief that the entire Arctic Circle was legally the same thing.

Months passed before anyone realized "there appears to be no statutory authority for the appointing of a temporary judge" to preside over an NWT crime in the Yukon.[1] The wet blanket was the Northwest Territories Act, which mandated the territory's crimes be prosecuted within its borders.[2]

Moving the trial back to the NWT held little appeal — travel was too difficult, and there were no facilities and no media access. The Department of Justice reasoned that if a legislative act could prohibit a temporary court, another act could permit one. Bill 7 was hastily drafted and sent before the House of Commons, where it quickly passed before moving on to the Senate. After trimming an amendment to allow non-British subjects to serve on the jury, the Senate approved Bill 7 in late March, 1923.[3] The only thing keeping it from becoming law was the signature of Lord Julian Byng, the governor general of Canada. Byng was not in a signing mood, however, and the bill languished on his desk.

Lord Julian Hedworth George Byng, twelfth governor general of Canada (1921–1926).

Known to all as "Bungo," the nation's twelfth governor general frequently flouted tradition.[4] He travelled Canada far more widely than his predecessors, meeting with constituents of all creeds and ancestries. Byng also retooled the mandate of his post, which normally represented the interests of the Sovereign and British Government, in order to align himself with the Canadian people and their parliament.

Lord Byng often refused to sign bills that conflicted with his political beliefs, most notably during the 1924 "Byng-King Crisis" in which Byng refused to sign an Order-in-Council from Prime Minister William Lyon Mackenzie King seeking to dissolve Parliament. His refusal left Canada without a prime minister or government until Byng invited Arthur Meighen to form a governing body. One of Meighen's first orders of business was to issue an identical order seeking dissolution, a bill that Byng readily signed.[5]

Unlike with the King affair, Byng never publicly explained his reticence regarding Bill 7. In May, Judge Dubuc was appointed, even though the bill was still unsigned. Days before the judicial party was scheduled to depart for Herschel, the issue of jurisdiction was still not resolved. E.L. Newcombe sent a telegram to Irving Howatt acknowledging that Byng had yet to sign but instructing Howatt to "proceed in assumption that [the] bill has received assent."[6]

That telegram and hundreds like it reveal the excessive communication between the RCMP and Justice Department regarding this case. The bulging archival files contain no fewer than six memos urging the judicial party to pack sweaters for their impending trip north, yet nothing indicates the date Byng actually signed Bill 7, or that he signed it at all. Most importantly, there is no communiqué from Ottawa informing the judicial party the bill had become law. As Dubuc prepared to ascend the bench on Herschel Island, he took it on blind faith that his court was legally binding.

Regardless of when (or if) Lord Byng rendered Bill 7 into law, that crucial step came too late to legitimize one key aspect of the proceedings: the preliminary hearings.[7] A preliminary hearing does not assess the guilt or innocence of the accused; it determines whether enough evidence exists to move the case to trial. Every defendant charged with an indictable offence (including murder) has a right to a preliminary hearing.[8]

In November 1922, the RCMP appointed Inspector Wood to oversee those proceedings.[9] Whether the Mounties had the authority to make that decision is debatable, and the idea certainly had not come from the Justice Department. When Cory was appointed as defence counsel on May 16, 1923, the deputy justice minister assured him none of his clients had undergone a preliminary hearing, even though Wood had completed those hearings one month prior.[10]

Even Wood's boss came to question the legitimacy of the preliminaries. When Wood submitted his invoice for the hearings (claiming $1.50 per preliminary inquiry),[11] Commissioner Starnes refused to pay, arguing the accused men were committed for trial long before Wood held his kangaroo court.[12]

Timing was not the only concern, as issues of jurisdiction and geography once again reared their ugly heads. Wood was a justice of the peace for the Northwest Territories, an appointment giving him jurisdiction only within territorial boundaries. Wood held his preliminary hearings on Herschel Island in the Yukon, making those proceedings "invalid."[13]

It is a simple matter of law: if the preliminary hearing is invalid, the subsequent trial is also invalid.

Ten

Premeditation

On June 12, 1923, Justice Lucien Dubuc, prosecutor Irving Howatt, defence counsel Thomas Cory, and the remaining members of the judicial party boarded a railcar in Edmonton. The mood was light, the luggage was heavy, and the voyage had just begun. Their route north was strangled, proceeding by rail to Fort McMurray, then by schooner to Fort Smith, and finally down the Mackenzie River aboard the SS *Distributor* to Aklavik.

En route, the court party resembled an "Asiatic caravan, taking all their books, records, and impediments with them."[1] Given Dubuc's spendthrift tendencies, those footing the bill declared that "reasonableness and economy are to be the guiding principles" of the party's expenses.[2] Dubuc ignored the mandate, enjoying all the food, wine, and delights the transport allowed.

As Judge Dubuc boarded the A. & G.W. Railway car in Edmonton, the train's manifest contained two curious entries.[3] The first was a large load of lumber and rope. The cargo's final destination was Herschel Island. The second was a passenger, "Special Constable Gill," an RCMP officer "with carpentry experience."[4] Gill was a last-minute addition to the judicial party and the only man Dubuc had yet to meet.[5] The judge was uncertain of the man's role, but it did not take him long to find out.

No sooner had the train left the station than Gill revealed he had been hired as the hangman for Alikomiak and Tatamigana. Gill had been expressly

Cortlandt Starnes, the seventh commissioner of the RCMP (April 1, 1923–July 31, 1931). Born in Montreal on March 31, 1864, Starnes fought in the North-West Rebellion with the 65th Mount Royal Rifles Regiment before joining the North-West Mounted Police as an inspector in 1885.

ordered — by multiple people on several occasions — to keep quiet as to the specifics of his contract, but Gill was not known for his discretion.[6] "It is to be regretted," Gill's supervisor later admitted, "that this man's identity and the nature of his mission were discovered so early on the trip."[7]

The carpentry ruse was not entirely factitious; the RCMP had also contracted Gill to construct the gallows.[8] As for the lumber and rope in the baggage car, Gill was ordered to transport the necessary materials from Edmonton on the presumption there was no wood in the Arctic.

Special Constable Gill was the *nom de noose* of Fred L. Hill, a Montreal-based freelance executioner who came tepidly recommended by the city's sheriff. The Montreal sheriff had made the recommendation in secret, largely to prevent annoying Canada's official hangman, Arthur Ellis. The sheriff had mentioned Gill to Sergeant W.D.M. Henderson but had begged Henderson "not to let Ellis know that he had given me this man's address" for fear of reprisal.[9] Gill was not the RCMP's first or even second choice. Commissioner Starnes had first approached J.J. Wakelen,[10] the man who had successfully executed LeBeau in 1921.[11] Starnes offered Wakelen four dollars a day plus one hundred dollars per hanging.[12] Wakelen demanded five dollars, the going rate for "any provincial execution."[13] The hangman had no leverage and was so anxious to get the assignment that, when the commissioner balked, the hangman whispered he would do it for four dollars.

Wakelen initially accepted the job, but many in the RCMP had concerns.[14] He was "now an old man of 77," though still "very active for his age."[15] One year prior, Wakelen had almost missed the deadline for the LeBeau execution, arriving mere hours before the hanging was scheduled.[16] Starnes asked his men to discretely send out additional feelers.

The obvious choice was Arthur Ellis, Canada's official hangman. Ellis had a well-earned reputation for being difficult, however, and he had disappointed the Mounties in the past. Ellis was originally contracted to execute Albert LeBeau, but had turned back at Fort McMurray because he did not want to be trapped by the weather, forcing a retired Wakelen to step in at the last minute.

Ellis's fear of snow and his prima-donna attitude were on full display during his initial meeting with the RCMP, insisting, for example, that if the Mounties wanted to talk to him, they had to pay for his time and travel to Ottawa to discuss the matter in person.[17] The hangman declared he would consider taking the job, but only on the following conditions: "He wishes to go in with the judge, execute the prisoners immediately after sentence, and return with the judge's party."[18] He also wanted far more money than the force was prepared to pay.

Even if Starnes had been willing to meet his demands, Ellis was not available to do the job for months, as he already had multiple executions on his schedule.[19] With no other viable options, the RCMP offered the job to Gill.[20] Gill was in an excellent bargaining position, and he quickly talked the Mounties up to five dollars per day plus expenses and an additional five hundred dollars for each man hanged.[21] Starnes told his subordinates: "If Mr. Ellis calls again, you may intimate that … arrangements are being made to utilize the services of another man."[22]

Starnes resented Ellis, but he came to see the wisdom of his demands. Waiting for an actual verdict before sending a hangman to Herschel could delay the executions for a full year. Starnes decided Gill should act "as a Special Constable and go in with the party as such, being subject, of course, to the usual discipline and make himself generally useful as a carpenter in order that his identity might not be known until the time of the hanging."[23] When that time came, Gill would then "volunteer to do it, so to speak."[24] The ruse was necessary, Starnes reasoned, as there might be "a certain feeling amongst some against one performing that duty."

Starnes was right. Once on the island, Gill's often boorish behaviour, and his mere presence, made the locals so uncomfortable he was sent off-island to await his final duties. Gill was able to secure steady employment as a carpenter in Aklavik to fill the empty hours and line his pockets with extra cash.[25]

Gill was not the RCMP's preference, but neither was hanging. Given the presumed "scarcity of lumber," Commander Jennings suggested "it would be a matter of very great convenience and expediency if this could be changed to shooting."[26] His suggestion received serious consideration, but it was rejected because the noose was the only legal method of execution in Canada.[27]

Once on Herschel, Gill and a few local assistants went to work. They constructed the gallows in the abandoned bone shed previously used by whalers to dry their catches.[28] The building's peaked roof and dirt floor provided little clearance, and a certain amount of jerry-rigging was necessary. When the noose was tied and hung, Gill picked up a shovel and set to work on the graves.

None of Gill's preparations came as a surprise to those in authority, because it was always assumed the trials would end with executions. In a report written weeks before anyone south of 60 had learned of the murders, Inspector Wood argued the "executions should take place at Tree River for the sake of the example it will set."[29]

The chief prosecutor had the same thought. One week after his appointment, Howatt wrote to the Ministry of Justice. He never named the accused, referring to them only as "these people," but he insisted on "definite instructions concerning the sentences," specifically the death penalty.[30] A volley of letters ensued between Howatt, the DOJ and Dubuc, who joined the conversation via telegrams (sent collect and often in the wee hours of the morning). All missives focused on the mechanics of the executions, with little attention paid to "these people" or the substance of the case itself.[31]

Four days before Dubuc left Edmonton, he received a telegram from the deputy minister of justice instructing him to "consult police authorities as to the date and place of execution."[32] The verdict was now an open secret. Dubuc did as bidden, and Inspector Wood pushed for "the earliest possible execution date" because of the "depressing effect" any impending hangings would have on the tiny island community.[33]

The trials would be a mere formality. The message was what mattered: any Inuit who committed murder (particularly the murder of a white man) would be put to death. So entrenched was the notion of the monolithic North, however, that no one in a position of authority paused to consider how the Inuvialuktun speakers of Herschel Island were supposed to relay that message to the Inuinnaqtun speakers of Tree River 692 miles to the east.[34]

Eleven

Beyond Comprehension

As the hangman and judicial party were wending their way north, newly promoted RCMP Commissioner Cortlandt Starnes[1] was warned that, despite Inspector Wood's initial assurances, "there are not more than four British subjects competent to act [as jurors] all told" on Herschel Island.[2] Fearing a mistrial, Starnes gave Dubuc permission to recruit "such number of British subjects as may be considered necessary"[3] from anywhere the judge might find them. During a brief respite at Fort Norman, Dubuc conscripted two men to round out the panel.

After a solid month of travel, the now-fifteen-man judicial party arrived on Herschel Island on the morning of July 12, 1923. Alikomiak and his escorts had arrived earlier on a shuttle from Aklavik. The contingent from Tree River, including translator Cyril Uingnek; Binder's wife, Toktogan; and Tatamigana, had first landed at Aklavik on September 9, 1922.[4] Their journey by dogsled and schooner had lasted thirty-seven days.[5]

Inspector Wood did his best to ensure the comfort of his guests. Dubuc and the lawyers bedded down in the relative luxury of the Mission House. The jurymen and escorts were relegated to tents.[6] Alikomiak and Tatamigana were placed in the holding cell, although security was lax and the pair often wandered freely about the island.

The wooden RCMP barracks on Herschel Island, circa 1925. The cuisine on offer was simple, typically canned goods supplemented with local game. Judge Dubuc, ever gracious, commended Wood and his men on their hospitality.

Herschel's cavernous RCMP barracks would serve as the courthouse. The building was designed with an eye for function rather than grandeur. Absent were the theatrical flourishes of Dubuc's prior remote court. During the 1921 LeBeau trial, Dubuc had used the altar of a rococo Roman Catholic missionary chapel as his bench, backed by a billboard-sized Union Jack.[7] On Herschel Island, Dubuc would make due with a plain wooden chair on the floor of the sparse police barracks.

Lost in all the preparations and legal wrangling were the victims and their families. Corporal William Doak's siblings learned of his murder by reading about it in the newspaper. Doak's brother Allison sent a desperate letter to the RCMP on July 22, 1922. A Manitoba newspaper had just published an account of a "Corporal Boak of Herschel Island" killed by "Eskimos," and Allison was worried the dead officer was his brother. Cortlandt Starnes issued a generic reply disavowing any knowledge of the murder.[8]

Starnes's denial was disingenuous, as he had received confirmation of Doak's death one day prior.[9] On July 25, Starnes instructed the commander of the Winnipeg detachment to contact Doak's mother and "express my deep regrets at the death of her son."[10] The Doak family wrote back, informing Starnes his records were out of date; Doak's mother had died the year before in New Brunswick.[11]

The RCMP's prolonged ignorance of the corporal's death left an eerie trail of business-as-usual documentation in Doak's service file throughout the spring and summer of 1922.[12] One week after Starnes first learned of the death, he made another startling discovery: the force had continued to pay Doak after he was shot. On August 1, 1922, Starnes ordered Major Jennings to contact the manager of the Canadian Bank of Commerce in Edmonton and demand the bank "repay to us the amount representing his April, May, and June cheques," deposits totalling $225. Eight days later, Jennings replied the bank would not remove money from the dead man's account.[13]

The $225 became a sticking point for Starnes, who generated an impressive number of memoranda and letters trying to recoup the money.[14] The RCMP offered no compensation to families of officers killed in the line of duty; instead, the force filed a suit to ensure they would be repaid for the months it took them to learn of Doak's death.

The family repaid the $225, insisting they did not "care about his money." Instead, they wanted "some article of remembrance," specifically Doak's rifle, revolver, Stetson hat, and belt.[15] The RCMP sent the Stetson, but held on to Doak's service weapons.

Doak died without a will, leaving the force to deal with his personal effects. His worldly possessions fit inside a single "very old" suitcase containing nothing of value save for two watches.[16] Most items were "cheap ... probably intended to be traded with the natives." The timepieces and trinkets were released to the family; his uniform, toque, and fur cap were returned to the RCMP.

Upon first learning of Doak's demise, Starnes's initial response was "to hope that we will find there was no negligence or carelessness in this unfortunate business." His second thought was of vengeance. "I think it is about time a proper lesson should be given to the natives," he said, adding that any trials should be handled "quickly and effectively."[17] Starnes told the Justice Department there was no need to send a prosecutor to try Alikomiak for the crime, as such duties "can be handled quite satisfactorily" by his own men.

Starnes had great faith in his troops, but the Mounties no longer had anything good to say about Doak. The corporal had died in the line of duty, but the specifics of his passing — shot in the rear while sound asleep — did not lend itself to media glorification. Doak's superiors were quick to blame the victim. Like all northern officers, Doak had received explicit instructions never to be alone with the Inuit.[18] Major Jennings felt Doak "should have been doubly on his guard" because he was "handling a dangerous murderer, one to whom the value of a human life was nothing; one who a few days previously had deliberately killed his own uncle and was proud of it."[19]

Jennings also posthumously castigated Doak for failing to keep the men of the detachment together and for neglecting to secure all firearms in a locked location with "the keys put in a place unknown to the prisoner."[20] Jennings had no way of knowing whether that was true, as none of the RCMP's reports indicated whether the storeroom was unlocked when Woolams and Clarke first arrived at the scene (or any time thereafter), nor did anyone bother to note where the keys were after the shootings.

The force's official report on Doak's murder was equally harsh. "To be outspoken," the account concluded, "Corporal Doak took an unnecessary chance and lost out," adding, "of course, none of these particulars have been given to the Press or to Corporal Doak's relatives."[21]

While Doak's name was turned to mud, Binder's reputation was being burnished by many hands. The HBC had no grieving family to appease. The trader's nearest living relative — a brother employed by the Standard Oil Company — was stationed in Manilla.[22] The two had not spoken in years. The HBC believed the "rest of his people" lived somewhere in the American northwest, but Binder had no contact with them. The company ran ads in the Seattle newspapers asking next-of-kin to contact their headquarters, but they received no reply.

Binder also left no will. He owned little of any real worth, only a trunk "of no more value than $1.00," having "traded off most of his personal belongings while at Tree River." His Savage. 32 revolver was reclaimed by the company. The rest was given to Toktogan but she "left whatever stuff was handed over to her" at the Tree River outpost.[23]

The company felt no obligation to give Toktogan anything. "Binder was not legally married to the woman nor did he go through any form of marriage with her," an HBC spokesman argued, concluding, "she has no claim upon Binder or his estate."[24]

The company dismissed Binder's relationship with Toktogan, but those in Kent Peninsula did not. When Toktogan left her husband Ikialgagina to partner with Binder, Ikialgagina went in search of a new mate. The unrest that followed culminated in Pugnana's killing spree.[25] Despite hearing witness testimony to that effect, Corporal Doak had put the blame firmly on Ikialgagina, a "useless troublemaker [who] could not keep a wife when he had one."[26] By the time Doak had completed his official report on the Kent Peninsula massacre, all reference to Toktogan and Binder's relationship had been erased.

The Honourable Company expressed their gratitude for Doak's careful rewriting of history, stating: "It is a pleasure to note that the report ... does not connect Binder with the regrettable affair."[27]

Twelve

A More Likely Story

Inspector Stuart Wood was a very busy man. In addition to the preparations needed to host the historic court trials, there was the criminal investigation central to the trials. As the region's resident commander, it fell to Wood to gather the necessary evidence.

The foundation of the Crown's case was the police report prepared by Corporal J.H. Bonshor. Like Doak before him, Wood had, during his first review of the file, diligently scrubbed any reference to Binder's relationship from the records regarding the two murders at Tree River. Even so, there were still too many holes, inconsistencies, and failings of logic in the investigative report for the inspector's liking.[1] With the trials slated to begin, Wood took matters into his own hands.

The problem, Wood decided, rested with Bonshor, whose "investigation and report on this murder is far from satisfactory, in fact in some instances his statements are entirely wrong."[2] Bonshor's report included the interrogation of the accused. Alikomiak had given two official statements to police, confessions that would come back to haunt them. The troublesome issue was motive: "It might appear to some that there was some provocation for Alikomiak killing Cpl. Doak, in that he states Cpl. Doak threatened him with the dog whip."[3]

A portrait of Inspector Stuart T. Wood, taken by Knud Rasmussen's team during the fifth Thule expedition of 1924–1925. Rasmussen described Wood as "a keen and capable man, fully alive to the difficulties of maintaining law and order" in the North.

Such a threat was grounds for self-defence and acquittal, a situation Wood sought to avoid. "I have therefore seen fit to take another statement from Alikomiak," Wood told his superiors, assuring them they would be pleased with the result as it "throws more light on the case and explains many things."[4]

Wood's interrogation of the prisoner removed any trace of the self-defence argument. According to Indigenous scholars, Alikomiak's contemporaries believed it was possible to "kill people" with your voice.[5] Northern police were routinely instructed never to threaten the locals or appear angry, as the "Inuit believed that a man who spoke harshly had it in his mind to commit murder, and that it was thus reasonable and proper to kill him first."[6] Alikomiak's newly revised statement, reshaped by Wood's guiding hand, portrayed Doak as a calm, non-threatening man who "spoke more in an ordinary tone of voice."[7]

With self-defence off the table, Wood introduced his own theory: suicide-by-cop. Wood told his superiors, "The whole point is that Alikomiak did not want to be taken west to Herschel Isl., and he was quite willing to go to any extreme and if necessary die rather than do so."[8] In Wood's version of events, Alikomiak no longer intended to kill the officer, meaning only to wound him and give Doak "a chance to get his revolver which was hanging beside the bed."

Wood also cleaned up the "other discrepancies" in Bonshor's crime report that were "at once noticeable." Bonshor stated Doak's wound was to the right buttock, an observation echoed by Woolams and Clarke in their initial statements. This detail conflicted with Alikomiak's claim that Doak was laying on his right side with his face to the wall and therefore could not see him coming. Wood nixed the prior accounts, moving Doak's injury from the right to left buttock in his final report. Wood went on to alter or remove other significant details from the previous statements, including which rifle was used as the murder weapon.[9]

Alikomiak's third confession introduced Western concepts, such as a strict accounting of time and imperial measures, which could only have come from Inspector Wood. One of Wood's chief complaints about Bonshor's report was that it lacked specificity. Bonshor had accepted Alikomiak's vague recollections as to the mechanics of the shootings. By the time Wood was finished, Alikomiak had sworn he was "to the left of the stove and about three feet from it," and that he shot Doak from a distance of ten feet,[10] despite having no experience with such systems of measurement.

Wood later forced the testimony of all Inuit witnesses to conform to the twenty-four-hour clock. Alikomiak and Toktogan's first statements expressed Inuit notions of time such as "soon" or "the sun was high." Such imprecision could not be integrated into the timeline generated by white witnesses like Woolams or Clarke. In the final statements overseen by Wood, the Inuit began anchoring specific events to temporal landmarks such as 8 a.m., despite having little familiarity with clocks or measured time.

The clearest evidence of Wood's tampering occurred in the addendum to Alikomiak's statement. Three people were involved in recording the confession: Alikomiak recounting his experience; Cyril Uingnek translating both the questions and answers; and Wood asking the questions and typing the responses on the RCMP witness form. Despite Cyril's best efforts, the narrative was in pidgin English — grammatically incorrect with little regard for tense, punctuation, or syntax. After struggling through two hours of testimony[11] and filling the form with sentence fragments and typos, Alikomiak supposedly ended his voluntary statement by declaring: "I have been warned that anything I may say can be used against me at my trial and that I am not bound to say anything now or later."[12] Wood could have noted he had given the warning, but he chose to put the words in Alikomiak's mouth. Alikomiak was then made to sign a confession he could not read, marking his name with an X.

Wood's tinkering with the statement created more logical inconsistencies than it resolved. If Alikomiak intended to commit suicide by the hand of another, why did he shoot Binder? There was also the lingering question of why Doak had not returned fire after Alikomiak shot him. The corporal had his gun within reach and plenty of opportunity. "Doak was evidently conscious for some time after being shot," Wood noted, "and it may have been all of two hours before he died."[13] If Doak was conscious so long, why did he not shoot when Alikomiak came back into the room? Even if Doak feared he could no longer save himself, why had he not protected Binder when Alikomiak openly stalked the trader as he approached the barracks? By the same token, when it was clear the first shot had not killed Doak, and Doak had not returned fire, why did Alikomiak not shoot him again?

Once completed, no one other than Inspector Wood and Cyril Uingnek knew what the revised statements contained. Although Wood had informed Starnes of his activities, the statements were not included in his communiqués south. Howatt did not see the reworked statements (or any statements) until he set foot on Herschel Island. Prior to and throughout the trials, the Department of Justice and Commissioner Starnes had no direct communication with the judicial party and had no idea what was taking place on Herschel. Starnes conceded he knew only "what has appeared in the press."[14]

In Wood's defence, his tampering seemed driven by a desire to deliver a solid case for the prosecution rather than by malice or malignant racism. His attitude toward the Inuit was no better or worse than the social norm. If Wood suffered from anything, it was a rampant case of confirmation bias, leading him to see only what supported his preconceived notions of the case. In Wood's view, he had done nothing improper by retooling the statements and the report. Alikomiak had confessed, not once, but three times.

Thirteen
An Unfortunate Choice of Hobby

Despite the pretrial frenzy, Judge Dubuc found time to pursue his favourite leisure activity: photography. He carried his camera to Herschel to capture his experiences for posterity, just as he had during the LeBeau trial in Fort Providence.[1] Already certain of his place in history, Dubuc wanted to ensure such histories would be well-illustrated.

Some of his photographs inadvertently recorded evidence of his legal improprieties and lapses in judgment.

While on Herschel, Dubuc frequently broke from standard judicial procedure or abandoned it altogether. For instance, there was no voir dire. The ten-man jury was hand-picked by Dubuc and the panel was as white as the winter landscape. The jury was "packed" with "superior" social status individuals who were "receptive to instructions from the bench."[2] The judge believed the Indigenous people could not comprehend, much less apply, the fundamentals of British justice.

The Inuit were also "godless," a situation Dubuc intended to remedy by example according to what he considered his "proselytizing responsibilities."[3] "We want it plainly understood in the minds of these people," Dubuc claimed, "that one of our most important laws is for the protection of human life which flows from the Divine Commandment 'Thou shall not kill.'"[4]

Justice Dubuc in a casual moment on Herschel Island, July 1923.

The judge rationalized his jury choices by stating the panel was "selected with the advice of the local Police Authorities, having regard to their knowledge of the ways and customs of the Eskimo."[5] Sharing the blame did not temper the fact that such a demographically skewed panel — known colloquially as jury-packing and legally as embracery — was a punishable offence in Canada.[6]

Dubuc showed little concern for any downstream ramifications of his decision as he explored the shoreline of Herschel Island. He was too busy playing tourist, always in the company of others, camera in hand to record those carefree moments. The company he kept was often problematic. While there is nothing unusual or unethical about friendships between judges and the lawyers or bailiffs in their courts, Dubuc repeatedly crossed

Lucien Dubuc, far left, as he gathered with the locals near Aklavik to witness a whale hunt, early July 1923. Among those posing with the judge is Tatamigana (second from right), the accused man destined for Dubuc's courtroom.

a crucial line by socializing with two off-limits groups: jurors, and the accused.

Dubuc was frequently seen, and photographed, enjoying amiable moments with Alikomiak and Tatamigana. The accused men shared cigarettes and smiles with the judge, and were granted moments of liberty to explore their surroundings with their new friend.

Another of Dubuc's island friendships violated the same ethical guidelines, as well as a few statutes. As the judicial party passed through Fort Norman on June 24, 1923, Dubuc had recruited a local resident named Paul S. Poirier to serve as a juryman.[7]

Dubuc and Poirier struck up a friendship as the party continued north. For whatever reason — maybe Dubuc liked Poirier's moxie, or perhaps the judge was still smarting from the justice minister's slashing of his retinue — Dubuc hired Poirier to serve as his secretary.[8] Once on Herschel, Dubuc also empaneled Poirier as a member of the jury. That action in itself was grounds for Dubuc's disqualification and censure, as Poirier was already serving as a member of the court.[9]

More violations were to come. Poirier began taking copious notes, which he later crafted into a lengthy article and sold to a series of newspapers.[10] The subheading of his piece proclaimed he had "acted as secretary

Judge Dubuc (on the right) and Paul S. Poirier exploring the local village on Herschel Island, early July 1923. Several photos reveal the judge and juror shared friendship and frequent communications outside the confines of the courtroom.

for Judge Dubuc at the recent Eskimo murder trials," and was therefore privy to the inner workings of the court.[11] This was a breach of his oath as a juror not to discuss the case with any outside party — an offence punishable by fine, imprisonment, or both.[12] Although Poirier's article was published after the trial ended, he invoiced the court for a total of sixty-one days as a juror and swore an oath that such time was spent "entirely on the public service."[13]

Poirier profited handsomely from his time on Herschel. In addition to his secretarial salary from Dubuc, he collected five dollars per day plus expenses and per diems as a juror, as well as whatever compensation he received for his newspaper reportage. Although Dubuc and Poirier's malfeasance is easily spotted in retrospect, no one noticed at the time, and the pair escaped all recrimination.

On the morning of July 16, 1923, Dubuc's camera captured a moment the judge had taken great care to stage.[14] The picture shows the entire Herschel Island judicial party arranged in front of the RCMP barracks. Dubuc stands proudly in the centre, flanked by the lawyers, bailiffs, and court officers. Alikomiak, Tatamigana, and the other accused Inuit were made to pose at the feet of the men brought north to prosecute them.

The judicial party for the Herschel Island trials poses in front of the RCMP barracks, July 1923. Dubuc's handwritten notations on the archival photo identify 1) RCMP Sergeant Spriggs, police escort, 2) Inspector Stuart Wood, 3) Constable Perry, police escort, 4) RCMP translator Cyril Uingnek, 5) Crown Prosecutor Irving Brass Howatt, 6) Judge Lucien Dubuc, 7) Defence Counsel Thomas Lewis Cory, 8) Dubuc's secretary and juryman Paul S. Poirier, 10) Constable Greville of the Herschel Island detachment, 11) Tatamigana, and 12) Alikomiak. Individuals marked 9, 13, and 14 were Inuit accused of various crimes and tried in separate trials (all were acquitted or given short jail sentences). The three men to the right of Cory in the back row are Special Constable Gill (a.k.a. the hangman Fred A. Hill) and his assistants.

No doubt Dubuc intended the photo as a solemn remembrance of a historically significant moment, but his decision to include everyone was regrettable. As the camera's aperture clicked, three men in the back row — "Special Constable Gill" and his local assistants — were caught making bunny ears and other irreverent hand gestures behind each other's heads. In retrospect, it is the perfect tone-deaf image of a show trial that was fast becoming a travelling circus.

III: TRIAL BY ERROR

The Eskimo, especially when he or one of his fellows has admitted killing a white man, finds it extremely difficult to understand why the red-coated mounted policeman, representative of the white man's law, should not shoot him on sight, but instead should bring him out to civilization where a big white chief, dressed like a woman, sits on a bench and hears another white chief say, on the Eskimo's behalf, that though he killed the white man in question, he should not be punished.

— *Winnipeg Evening Tribune*, October 31, 1922

Fourteen

All Evidence to the Contrary

At precisely 10 a.m. on July 16, 1923, Judge Dubuc gavelled in his inaugural Arctic court. The local Inuit had been hastily assembled "to witness the strange and awful workings of the white man's law."[1] The humble setting did little to dampen the solemnity of the event or the awe it inspired in those mandated to watch. A courtroom observer noted that, as Dubuc entered the room, "wonderment [was] written all over their dangerous looking yet friendly faces."[2]

The first case on the docket was *King v Tatamigana*, who was charged with five counts of murder for the shooting affray on Kent Peninsula. In a last-minute bid to secure convictions, Howatt reduced the charges to two counts of shooting with the intent to kill.

No witness lists were submitted by either side and there is no evidence of any discovery process. Nothing indicates Cory ever met with his clients before trial. Less than twenty-four hours before the gavel dropped, Howatt recognized the gaps in procedure and scratched out vague indictments so that formal charges could be read at the beginning of trial.[3] Despite Howatt's Hail-Mary efforts, surviving court records clearly indicate Dubuc relied solely on Wood's geographically invalid preliminary hearings as the basis for proceeding to trial.[4] Thomas Cory could (and should) have submitted a writ of habeas corpus — a doctrine protecting prisoners against unlawful

Tatamigana at the RCMP barracks awaiting his turn in the dock, July 1923. Although Herschel was chosen because it had a holding cell, the accused spent little time locked in detention.

detention and the basis for challenging the jurisdiction of a court[5] — before the trials began, but Cory was not working in his clients' best interests.[6]

No transcript of Tatamigana's first trial remains, although the proceedings were recorded in police reports and media accounts.[7] Tatamigana's statement, in which he freely confessed to the crime, was the sole evidence admitted. The trial was brief, with only a handful of witnesses called.

The jury deliberated twenty-five minutes before returning a verdict of guilty on the first count (relating to the death of Hannak) but not guilty on the second count (the death of Ikputuwak.) Judge Dubuc moved directly to the penalty phase, sentencing Tatamigana to five years in the Herschel Island lock-up.[8]

The trial had been staged for the benefit of the local people, but the performance was lost on its intended audience. The adversarial tone of the proceedings bewildered the Inuit, long-accustomed to a more consensus-driven approach to justice.[9] Translator Cyril Uingnek tried to convey the gist of the hearing, but it was clear neither the accused nor the gallery understood what had transpired. The locals were also confounded by Tatamigana's inability to speak on his own behalf. At the time, Canadian law prohibited defendants from addressing the court, whereas modern Inuit scholars insist traditional law offered ample opportunity for the accused to defend themselves.[10]

The next morning, the docket focused on the separate trials of Tatamigana and Alikomiak, each charged with murder in the September 1921 shooting of Pugnana. Tatamigana's trial consumed the morning. Only two witnesses were called: Inspector Wood, to admit the accused's confession; and Alikomiak, who described the plot to kill Pugnana as well as the actual shooting. Dubuc allowed the prosecutor to lead witnesses "atrociously."[11] Howatt later admitted as much in a confidential letter to the justice department. He complained that the Inuit's primitive "stage of development" and "entire lack of knowledge on court procedure" made eliciting intelligent testimony impossible. Wrote Howatt: "When you get them away from pure narrative of their own experience, the only way you can get an intelligent answer is to put a direct leading question, but as I said before, I always obtained permission from the Judge before putting such a question."[12]

The defence called no witnesses and the jury deliberated a mere eight minutes. The panel returned with a guilty verdict, tempered with a "strong recommendation for mercy."[13]

Alikomiak's trial took up the better part of the afternoon. Again, the dock held only two witnesses: Wood, reprising his role as the bearer of the accused's confession; and Tatamigana, repaying the favour done to him at the morning's proceedings. Jurors deliberated for nineteen minutes — most of it spent filling in the necessary paperwork — before delivering their guilty verdict with the same recommendation for mercy.[14] Dubuc announced he would delay sentencing in both trials until a later date.

....................——————————....................

Thomas Cory had sworn an oath to defend his clients vigorously, but he failed to raise a crucial issue: the Inuit had their own system of justice. While Canadian jurisprudence views murder as a crime to be punished, Inuit law treats murder as a tragedy to be avenged.[15] Under their own law, Tatamigana and Alikomiak were simply righting a wrong by killing Pugnana. Today, Inuit legal scholars such as Aupilaarjuk et al. concur. Taking out "an angry or insane person" who posed a threat to the band was considered a legitimate act.[16] The same held true for the massacre at Kent Peninsula. Tatamigana claimed the victims were "not good hunters and they were always causing trouble. I am sure they would have killed a lot of people if they had not been killed first."[17] That Alikomiak and Tatamigana remained valued members of the band after the murder suggests the community was complicit in the act. This was a notion Cory avoided at all costs.

....................——————————....................

Two days in, Dubuc's historic court was already awash in procedural and ethical violations. Some predated the actual trial, most notably the actions of Inspector Wood. At the time of his preliminary hearings, Wood wore many hats: RCMP inspector, justice of the peace, and coroner, as well as being a newly appointed "Deputy Sheriff in and for the Northwest Territories."[18] Wood tried his best to juggle his varying responsibilities, but conflicts were inevitable.

On April 17, 1923, Wood took Alikomiak's statement in his capacity as an RCMP peace officer investigating the murders of Binder and Doak.[19] Wood then admitted that statement to himself as justice of the peace at the preliminary hearing one week later — a clear conflict of interest and grounds for his disqualification as presiding justice.[20]

During their preliminary hearings, Alikomiak and Tatamigana were unrepresented by counsel. According to Wood, "no defence was put in" at the hearings and no one protected their interests or guided them through the bewildering labyrinth of Canadian jurisprudence.[21] They were stripped of their constitutional right to cross-examine witnesses at their preliminaries because such interrogation could only be done through lawyers.[22] Wood claimed to have warned the prisoners pursuant to the Criminal Code of Canada, although what that meant was unclear. To this day, the RCMP does not have a universal caution,[23] and the statute governing a prisoner's rights was not enacted until 1982.[24] Whatever counsel or cautions Wood offered the prisoners never rose to the level of having a dedicated defence lawyer, and Alikomiak and Tatamigana had no way of knowing where their statements would eventually lead them.

Wood's preliminary hearings also neglected another vital step: neither Alikomiak nor Tatamigana entered a plea.[25] Had either pled guilty — a very real possibility, given the number of times each supposedly confessed to their crimes — the law required the court move directly to sentencing. Such an outcome would have robbed the government of their much-needed show trial. It was a risk Wood could not take, but in so doing he violated the accused's rights to due process.

Wood put little stock in due process and had seemingly even greater contempt for forensic science. His officers failed to fingerprint Alikomiak or Tatamigana, disregarding Wilfrid Laurier's 1908 Executive Order making fingerprints the official Canadian standard for identifying criminals.[26] Wood saw no use for such prints as he made no attempt to link the suspects to the alleged murder weapons via fingerprints, even though the method had been in common use since 1877.

Authorities also neglected to autopsy the victim and recover the bullet. The unique grooves on projectiles caused by the firing pin and barrel — known as rifling — are as distinctive as a fingerprint and had successfully been used to match a spent bullet to a specific weapon since 1900.[27]

Wood did recognize the need to gather some physical evidence. He planned to go to Tree River in the late summer of 1922 "to obtain further details on this case and collect the exhibits," but was sidetracked by

Corporal William Doak (on the left) and Constable Woolams on patrol, December 1921. The photo was taken as Doak and Woolams headed to Kent Peninsula to investigate the June massacre. The image proves Doak had access to a camera during his patrol, yet no photos of the crime scene, victim's body, or any other evidence were taken — another example of the best evidence rule being ignored.

Alikomiak's arrival in Aklavik.[28] Wood instructed the remaining officers at Tree River as to "what future evidence to look for and obtain," but nothing tangible arrived at Herschel Island. Even Doak understood the significance of an autopsy and had intended to make another patrol to Kent Peninsula to recover Pugnana's body, but his untimely death derailed the plan.

Wood's apathy toward forensic evidence was bested only by that of the prosecutor. The only exhibits entered at trial were the confessions. The jury never saw the murder weapons or any depictions of the scene or victim. There was no analysis of blood patterns, footprints, or ballistics. Howatt saw no need for science, and the verdicts vindicated his approach; the confessions alone were enough to secure the necessary convictions. Howatt's disdain for forensic science may have been a successful legal strategy, but it was also a flagrant violation of the rule of best evidence, which requires "the most persuasive evidence available" be used to prove any relevant fact.[29]

Howatt left a lot of best evidence at the courtroom door. When Doak first arrested Alikomiak and Tatamigana for Pugnana's murder, he rounded up key witnesses: Anagvik and his spouse, as well as Pugnana's disabled wife. When the HBC supply schooner made its annual rounds to Tree River that fall, Inspector Wood ordered the witnesses to be put aboard and brought to Herschel Island to testify. For reasons never made clear, the witnesses were left standing on shore.[30] Physical evidence was also left gathering dust. Police reports indicated Alikomiak had shot Doak using a gun "which was an exhibit in one of the murder cases" from the June massacre, but the rifle never made it into the courtroom during either trial.[31]

The best-evidence doctrine was not the only legal concept Howatt overlooked. Corpus delicti — "the body of the crime" — refers to the "ingredients of the offence," such as the corpse of a murdered person.[32] The corpus delicti rule of criminal law prohibits prosecution based solely on a defendant's confession.[33] The Crown must independently establish the elements of the crime through other means, such as witnesses or physical evidence. Failure to do so is solid grounds for appeal and would almost certainly lead to the vacating of a verdict.

The Crown's sidestepping of the corpus delicti was as masterful as it was egregious. To secure a murder conviction, the Crown must offer concrete evidence that the victim once lived and had died at the hands of another. That is why autopsies are performed in all unnatural deaths and why the medicolegal authority must positively identify all remains through accepted scientific means. In prosecuting Tatamigana and Alikomiak for the murder of Pugnana, Howatt missed three crucial steps: he never proved a man named Pugnana existed, nor did he offer any proof Pugnana had died, much less of unnatural causes. Instead, Howatt jumped straight to the whodunit, correctly believing the jury would fill in the blanks for themselves.

The prosecutor certainly had other options. He could have called members of Pugnana's band to testify as to his existence or death. Doak's death had removed him from the witness list, but Constable Woolams was present during the investigation. Although Woolams was already in the courtroom, Howatt left him sitting in the gallery. The prosecution could have also admitted Doak's investigative report as a traditional exception to the hearsay rule, giving jurors some sense of Pugnana's existence, but Howatt saw no need.[34]

The Crown also failed to prove Pugnana was dead or offer evidence as to how he died. Neither Doak nor Woolams had seen his remains because his burial place was covered with snow when the RCMP first investigated.

Howatt's trampling of the corpus delicti rule was not inadvertent; he needed to perform legal backflips in order to do it.[35] In the bowels of the national archives rests an unsigned and incomplete carbon copy of a memo dated December 2, 1922. The memo was generated by the RCMP, although its author remains unknown.[36] The missive details various means of circumventing existing statutes in order to prosecute the accused Inuit. There was little chance of any blowback for such machinations. Cory was sympathetic to the government's cause and, as Commissioner Starnes privately joked, the Inuit prisoners "do not understand our laws and hardly realize why they have been arrested and sentenced."[37]

Alikomiak and Tatamigana were originally charged as co-conspirators in the murder of Pugnana. The anonymous memo pointed out that if they were "charged jointly with the killing," they could not be "compelled witnesses."[38] Howatt had no power to compel Alikomiak or Tatamigana to testify against each other. In such cases, the prosecution typically cuts a deal with the lesser offender — in this case, Tatamigana — to turn evidence against the trigger man. Howatt could have named Tatamigana as an unindicted conspirator in exchange for his testimony, but Tatamigana would have escaped all punishment for the crime. Instead, Howatt used the accused men's complete lack of legal knowledge — and Cory's apathy — to coerce their testimony.

At the time, defendants could not testify on their own behalf and co-defendants could not testify against each other. One conspirator recounting his conversation with another technically constitutes hearsay. While U.S. law recognizes a co-conspirator exception to the hearsay rule, Canadian law does not.[39] The prosecutor heeded the memo's advice and split the charges.[40]

In so doing, Howatt had followed the letter of the law but violated its intent, setting the stage for an even greater legal travesty. Alikomiak and Tatamigana were forced to testify against each other within hours on the same day before the exact same jury panel, in effect confessing to their own culpability. Any competent defence attorney would have stopped such blatant self-incrimination, but Cory never raised an objection.

Howatt disregarded the concepts of corpus delicti and best evidence, but there were safeguards in place that should have stopped him. Wood should have recognized the utter lack of physical and supporting evidence at the preliminary hearings. Dubuc had an obligation to uphold standards and ensure that basic legal elements were met at trial. Cory could have filed a motion to dismiss, arguing the prosecution had not met its burden of proof.

The Department of Justice and the governor general also shared in the blame, as their review of the case was mandated by law and was the closest thing Alikomiak and Tatamigana had to an appeal of their convictions. That no one noticed the gross violations of criminal procedure suggests incompetence or indifference at best, willful malfeasance at worst.

Fifteen

Ineffective Counsel

Alikomiak stood trial for the murders of Doak and Binder on the morning of July 18. During a brief pretrial motion, Cory tried to have his client's confession thrown out, but his objection was overruled.[1] The court personnel remained the same save for one: Johnny Tokluk stepped in as translator, freeing Cyril Uingnek to testify.

The first witness called to the stand was Inspector Wood. After taking the oath, Wood produced two pale-blue sheets of paper. In preparation for his preliminary hearings, Wood told the court he had interrogated Alikomiak, typing out the statement as Cyril translated the accused's confession. As his typing was quite poor, the blue witness form was riddled with typos, and Wood begged the court's indulgence as he read the statement aloud. He then handed it to the court clerk, Sergeant Wild, who admitted it into evidence as exhibit one.

By this stage, Wood's continuous presence in the courtroom had lulled the reporters in the gallery into a stupor, but a casually dispensed snippet of information soon roused their attention. The furor surrounded jury member C.H. Clarke.

Clarke had been a friend of Otto Binder, reason enough to exclude him from the jury. Clarke had also been at Constable Woolams's side when he examined the crime scene, and had given police several statements to that effect, another disqualifying attribute. Clarke had already testified before Inspector Wood at the preliminary hearing in April — strike three against Clarke's suitability as a juror — but Howatt chose not to call him during the actual trial. When Clarke complained of making the long journey from Tree River for nothing (and was no longer eligible for compensation as a witness), Dubuc seated Clarke as a five-dollar-per-day juryman. The judge did not notice (or chose to overlook) the obvious conflicts of interest.

During the interrogation with Wood, Alikomiak stated he had travelled to the seal camp to kill the remaining white men in the region, naming Clarke as one of his intended targets. When Inspector Wood read that section in open court, all eyes turned to Clarke in the jury box. Dubuc could no longer deny he had a problem and was forced to remove Clarke from the panel.[2]

Dubuc's error haunted him long after the trial ended. When the judge eventually returned to civilization, he found his humiliation played out in the pages of the *Edmonton Journal*. The next day, as Clarke's invoice for jury service crossed his desk for approval, Dubuc arbitrarily cut $290 from his pay. Although he had rubber-stamped Poirier's triple-dipping during the trial, the judge could not bring himself to pay Clarke for a mistake of Dubuc's own making.[3]

The next witness, Constable Daniel Woolams, would be seated in the dock twice during the day's proceedings. His initial testimony provided little of direct substance to the case, but when Howatt recalled him to the stand, Woolams delivered. He painted a visceral picture of the crime scene, recounting a blood-soaked room and a valiant officer shot down in his prime. Woolams then described the injuries each victim had sustained.

Cory rose to cross-examine, making much of the fact that no autopsies were conducted. Woolams said the bodies could not be transported out for examination because the sled dogs were starving and there was not enough feed to run a team. Cory scored a small victory by pointing out the dogs had survived the winter and had even managed to bring Woolams to Herschel in time to testify.

Howatt compensated for the lack of autopsies by calling Dr. Phillip E. Doyle, the RCMP's acting assistant surgeon for the region. Doyle recalled he had last examined Doak in August 1921, although if there was any documentation supporting Doyle's contention, it was not admitted into evidence at trial. Furthermore, Corporal Doak's RCMP service records contain no mention of any exam on or near that date. Under oath, Doyle declared the heavy-smoking corporal to be in "perfect" health.[4] When pressed to elaborate, Doyle claimed Doak's physique was so ideal his death could only have been caused by a bullet.

Cory found the doctor's certainty amusing, asking time and again how Doyle could draw such definitive conclusions without having seen the body. Each time Doyle simply replied: "I knew the man was in perfect health."[5] It was a scientifically untenable argument, but Doyle held his ground, leaving Cory to shrug and retake his seat.

The two remaining witness were Inuit: Binder's wife Toktogan, and Ayalegak, one of the fur traders who came to Tree River on April 1. Johnny Tokluk did his best to interpret, but the transcript reveals frequent breakdowns in communication.

After swearing an oath to a God he did not recognize, Ayalegak described the morning in question. He had entered the HBC post and asked to see Binder. Toktogan responded by pointing toward the RCMP barracks across the bay. According to the witness, Alikomiak then said: "It is no use to go over there now as the two white men have gone."[6] That testimony contradicted Ayalegak's prior statement in which he claimed not to have seen or spoken to Alikomiak until he found the accused sitting on a bed in the police barracks. No one noted the discrepancy at the time.

Ayalegak told the court he crossed the ice to the barracks, only to discover the bodies of Doak and Binder. The witness then recounted how he and his trading partner sat with Alikomiak sipping tea in the HBC house while Toktogan prepared to go home to the seal camp. His indifference and stoic recollection, deadened further by the act of translation, troubled many courtroom observers. Finding nothing to be gained, Cory declined to cross-examine.

Toktogan entered the dock and, despite being called by the prosecution, Howatt often treated her as a hostile witness. He asked convoluted and leading questions, allowing him to effectively testify on her behalf. Cory never voiced a single objection. Howatt also berated Toktogan, ordering her to "think again" whenever her answer was not what he wanted. Toktogan retreated into silence, answering fewer questions as the pummelling continued. A frustrated Howatt tendered the witness with a wave of his hand.[7]

When the defence counsel rose to cross-examine this witness, his questioning served only to muddy the waters and aid the prosecution.

Thomas Lewis Cory posing with a local landmark while en route to Herschel Island. Photographed by Lucien Dubuc, June/July 1923. Named after his paternal grandfather, Thomas was the eldest of three children born to William and Laura (née Watson).

Cory had no experience as a criminal lawyer; he was chosen for his beliefs and not his talent.[8] His interests aligned perfectly with those of the Justice Department, and Deputy Minister Newcombe felt certain Cory would not become overzealous in his defence of the accused.[9] Cory's performance in the courtroom exceeded Newcombe's wildest expectations.

Justice Dubuc was of two minds regarding Cory's abilities. In court, Dubuc had surprisingly harsh words for the defence, declaring Cory to be "highly inexperienced, having no familiarity with jury trials." The judge lessened the sting by adding, "I am sure a brilliant career is open to him," at some future date far removed from the case at hand.

The judge was more magnanimous in his private correspondence.[10] Any shortcomings were not Cory's fault, Dubuc argued, and he "defended the accused to the best of his abilities, but his efforts were obviously curtailed by the previous admissions and confessions of the prisoners."

Dubuc also commended Cory for being a good soldier "who acted with all the professional ethics expected of him." Whatever Cory's faults, he was instrumental in achieving the government's desired outcome, and the judge praised him accordingly: "In the hands of a less scrupulous lawyer there would probably have been an acquittal in likely each of these Eskimo cases, and this expensive expedition would have ended in a gigantic fiasco and miscarriage of justice."

Legal scholars have since argued that a miscarriage of justice is precisely what Cory delivered, claiming his "performance, in sum, was lamentable."[11] Consensus holds that Cory's "criminal defence skills were negligible," his cross-examinations were "neither incisive nor crisp," and his questions were "aimless," as though he were "seduced by tangential issues."[12]

Critiques of his defence strategy read as a litany of things Cory failed to do. He should have argued Alikomiak was not a British subject and therefore not bound by his Majesty's laws. He also could have requested a change of venue, allowing Alikomiak to be tried by his true peers.

Cory also failed to object — or even notice — when the prosecution presented no fewer than three different motives for the murders of Binder and Doak. The first was introduced by Inspector Wood, who suggested Alikomiak was trying to commit suicide-by-cop.[13] Wood pointed to a section of the accused's most recent confession in which Alikomiak stated: "I wanted to wound him as there was a revolver beside his bed and I did not care if he shot me."[14] Wood offered a second, conflicting motive when he later testified Alikomiak had killed Doak and Binder because he "did not want to go west to Herschel Island." Woolams then introduced a third motive that explained both murders: Alikomiak wanted to kill all the white men in the region to avoid punishment for the murder of Pugnana. That Alikomiak had no understanding he might be punished for murder under Canadian law was lost on those making the argument.

Cory should have noticed there was no logical consistency to Alikomiak's actions given his supposed motivations. For instance, Alikomiak reportedly went to the seal camp with the intention of shooting Woolams and Clarke, yet en route Toktogan convinced him to unload his rifle and Toletuk later disarmed him completely. If he had already killed two white men and wanted to kill the rest, why was he so easily dissuaded?

Even Irving Howatt admitted he did not know what motivated Alikomiak and found his statements highly contradictory. The prosecutor dismissed the suicide-by-cop theory out of hand: "If Alikomiak were so desirous of death that he fired at Doak … it is difficult to see why he should shoot Binder dead."[15] Why would a suicidal man care who pulled the trigger so long as he ended up shot? Yet time and again, Cory ignored such incongruity, opting instead to lob softball questions at witnesses or refusing to cross-examine them altogether.

Most disturbing was Cory's failure to pursue Alikomiak's self-professed motive: he was frightened of Doak. Alikomiak had inadvertently raised the notion of self-defence when he spoke of Doak's physical and verbal abuse. Self-defence was a legitimate strategy, one which Toktogan had also raised in her statement to police when she claimed: "Alikomiak never mentioned that he had any intention to kill these men before." Toktogan had offered the defence a gift, but Cory rejected it.

Instead, the defence counsel floated a motive of his own. During his fleeting cross-examination of Toktogan he suggested she had hired Alikomiak to kill Binder. On cross-examination, Cory asked her: "Did you have Alikomiak work for you at the time and was [sic] you paying him?" Toktogan said no, and the matter was quickly dropped.

Having exhausted his witness pool, Howatt rested the prosecution's case. Cory rose briefly to announce the defence had no witnesses and no evidence to tender. Alikomiak was prohibited from testifying in his own defence, and Cory offered nothing to diminish the power of his client's repeated confessions.

Cory's blind faith in those confessions was shared by his contemporaries. Whatever legal shortcomings the case may have had, everyone's conscience was cleansed by the notion they were prosecuting the right man. That certainty has since been echoed by legal scholars and historians studying the case.[16] All agree the evidence was "overwhelming,"[17] and "there is no reason to suppose" Alikomiak's statements were untrue.[18]

Sixteen
Intermediate Targets

The court did not need to take Alikomiak's confession on faith. The forensic sciences were developed because eyewitness testimony is notoriously unreliable, including confessions.[1] Hard science is not meant to replace human recall in a court of law but rather to assess, support, or refute the stories being told by the witnesses.

Even with Inspector Wood's tweaking, and throughout all its versions and permutations, Alikomiak's account of the murders of Doak and Binder remained consistent regarding the basic events and their sequence: Just before dawn, Alikomiak stole a weapon from the gun lock-up. He entered the police barracks and shot Doak in the buttocks as he lay sleeping in his bed. A mortally wounded Doak was conscious and speaking for a prolonged period before he finally bled out, expiring just as Binder made his way across the ice toward the detachment. When Binder came within fifty yards, Alikomiak stood atop a chair, shouldered his own rifle — a 30-30 carbine[2] — and fired through the window,[3] striking an unsuspecting Binder in the chest and killing him instantly.[4] Alikomiak then ran to the HBC house and recruited Toktogan to help him drag Binder's body into the barracks.

Forensic scrutiny of that confession reveals four glaring inconsistencies. First, it is not possible to fire a gun through a window and accurately hit a target, particularly at a range of fifty yards. The glass pane

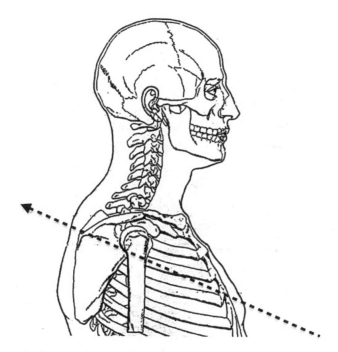

A schematic showing the wound track through Binder's body.

becomes an intermediate target, defined as any object the bullet passes through before striking its intended mark. The glass absorbs the bullet's energy and deforms the projectile, causing it to slow down and begin to "yaw" or wobble like a football at the end of a long pass, resulting in a dramatic change to its trajectory.[5]

In 1939, William W. Harper, a physicist and ballistics expert with the Pasadena Police Department, conducted a surprisingly specific and relevant experiment. Using a .38 service revolver, Harper had a trained marksman shoot through twenty panes of plate glass at a target positioned fifty yards from the glass panes. "No reliable data" was produced because the majority of the bullets missed the target completely, while the few that struck the stand missed the paper target by an average of nine inches.[6]

In the years since Harper's experiment, dozens of ballistic studies have reaffirmed his findings: bullets fired through glass do not hit their intended targets.[7] The notion that an inexperienced hunter like Alikomiak could fire through a glass window and kill Binder with a single shot to the heart at a range of fifty yards flies in the face of all modern ballistic science.

In fairness to Inspector Wood and his team, such science was not yet available to them. Ballistics was not admitted as evidence in court until 1929, although it was a recognized discipline in 1923.[8]

Ballistic expertise was not required to identify the second gross inconsistency: the flightpath of the shot that killed Binder did not line up. Reconstructing trajectory begins with the wound path. According to Woolams and Clarke, the bullet that killed Binder entered through the right breast just below the heart and exited out the right shoulder near the spine.[9] The bullet was travelling upward, exiting the body at a higher point than it entered, indicating the barrel of the gun was below Binder's heart and pointing up.

Alikomiak supposedly stood on a chair inside a building situated above the shoreline on the southern edge of the bay. Binder was walking on the ice. The RCMP barracks had to be well above the level of the water — otherwise it would have flooded every summer — which positioned Alikomiak's rifle far above the level of Binder's heart and pointing down.

A final point of reference completes the bullet's flight path. When Clarke examined the crime scene, he noted "the place where Binder had fallen was plainly marked where the Blood had seeped into the snow." Clarke also noticed "the mark of the bullet where it had plowed the snow at the rear of where Binder had been laying."[10]

For Alikomiak to have fired the bullet that killed Binder, that bullet had to pass through a glass intermediate target, travel fifty yards down the shoreline and across the ice, then suddenly veer upwards, strike Binder in the chest, exit out his upper back, then immediately veer downward, striking the snow behind where Binder was standing. Such a trajectory defies the laws of physics and gravity.

The third gross incongruity between Alikomiak's statements and the physical evidence concerns Binder's mental state at the time of his death. According to the accused, Binder had no idea he was being stalked. He was struck unawares, the bullet hitting his chest before the sound of the gunshot reached his ears.

Binder's body tells a different story. When Clarke and Woolams examined it, they noted his hands were clenched tight — a condition known as cadaveric spasm. Such spasms only occur in deaths "preceded by great

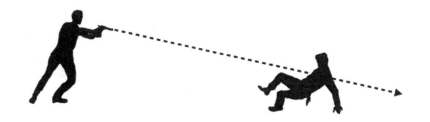

The most likely positional relationship between Binder (on the right) and his assailant. The same scenario applies if the shooter used a rifle; the assailant's stance would change slightly, but the flight path of the bullet and the wound track would remain the same.

excitement, fear or tension."[11] This instantaneous localized form of rigor mortis — commonly known as a death grip — is why many drowned people are found clutching seaweed and why homicide victims often have chunks of their assailant's hair or clothing locked tight in their fists. Cadaveric spasm does not occur in people struck down suddenly while walking on a morning visit to a friend.

The condition suggests Binder saw his assailant and knew what was coming. He was alone, unarmed, and defenceless on an open stretch of ice with nowhere to hide. His panic at the moment of his death was captured in his cadaveric spasms.

Collectively, Binder's wound track, the cadaveric spasm, and the bullet strike in the snow create an entirely new scenario. As Binder walked toward the RCMP barracks, his assailant moved toward him on the ice. Something about the assailant scared Binder — perhaps he knew his killer or maybe he saw the gun. Binder fell to the ground, either to plead for his life or to comply with his assailant's command. Binder's hands clenched in terror as he leaned away from his killer. The trigger was pulled and Binder lay dead, shot through the heart at a much closer range. The bullet's trajectory from the gun through Binder's body to where it landed in the snow behind him now align. Such a scenario explains the physical evidence of the scene and body far better than the tale told by Alikomiak.

Forensic analysis holds one final revelation: Binder died first, and not by mere minutes. In the 1920s, estimating time-since-death relied on the "triad" of postmortem changes: livor mortis (a purple discolouration of the skin caused by the settling of the blood); algor mortis (the progressive drop in body temperature); and rigor mortis (increasing rigidity of the muscles and joints). Each of the triad develops at a predictable rate during the first twenty-four hours after death, allowing investigators to determine when the victim died. The method is not capable of pinpointing the exact moment of death, but collectively the triad gives a reliable indication of the elapsed time-since-death.[12]

In their statements detailing their examination of Doak and Binder's bodies, Woolams and Clarke never mentioned skin discolouration or made any reference to lividity, but both men made observations of the body temperature and degree of rigor.

Putting a timeline to Alikomiak's statement is crucial. By including contributions from other witnesses, the following chronology emerges: Alikomiak said "the sun was just coming up" when he shot Doak.[13] Meteorological records indicate sunrise was at 6:29 a.m.[14] Doak survived approximately ninety minutes before succumbing to blood loss and shock moments before Binder was killed. Alikomiak knew only that he shot Binder "when the sun was high," but Toktogan said Binder made his fateful crossing of the bay at 8 a.m.[15] Binder died instantly of his wounds and Alikomiak ran across the ice to fetch Toktogan. The two Inuit then "dragged Binder into the house, he was quite dead, and covered him with a blanket." From that moment on (roughly 8:10 a.m.), the bodies of Doak and Binder were in the same ambient environment: covered by blankets in an uninsulated wooden police barracks, with a dying fire in the heat stove, and a broken window pane allowing frigid air into the room.[16]

Alikomiak and Toktogan then travelled to the seal camp, at which point Woolams learned of the murders. He recruited Clarke to accompany him to Tree River to investigate, leaving the seal camp at 3:15 p.m. and arriving at the RCMP barracks at just after 5 p.m. As they entered, the barracks was freezing, and the fire was completely extinguished.

When Woolams and Clarke examined the bodies, Binder and Doak had been dead for nine hours. The investigators stripped Doak of his covering and clothing, noting his wound and laying hands on his bare skin. Both men noted the body "was still warm and not rigid as yet." The pair then repeated the exercise with Binder's corpse. The trader "was rigid and the body was cold."

A number of factors can influence the rate of heat loss after death.[17] Exsanguination and blood-soaked clothing accelerate algor mortis, causing the body to cool faster than normal.[18] Doak "had bled freely and soaked the bed," while Binder's clothes showed little blood.[19] Doak's blood loss was greater because he had lived longer after being shot; his heart continued to pump and his blood remained under pressure, forcing it from the wound. Binder died almost instantly. With no beating heart to drive it, his blood loss was passive and minimal. Had both men died at roughly the same time, as Alikomiak claimed, Doak's body should have been colder than Binder's. Furthermore, after nine hours in a frigid room, neither Doak nor Binder should have registered as warm to the touch.[20]

The degree of rigor mortis tells a similar tale. Rigor becomes apparent within one hour of death and increases progressively until it reaches its maximum at twelve hours, at which point the entire body is as stiff as a plank.[21] Nine hours after death, Doak should have been as rigid and as tough to manipulate as Binder, but the corporal was like a rag doll.

Clarke attributed Binder's rigidity to the short time the trader spent laying on the ice, an erroneous interpretation. Cold environments actually delay rigor development; had he spent any significant time on the ice, Binder would have been less rigid than Doak. There was another telling indicator. After their examinations, Woolams and Clarke stretched the two dead men out flat and wrapped them in separate blankets. Clarke had to force Binder's limbs to straighten. Joints fixed by rigor can be flexed through forceful manipulation; frozen limbs cannot.[22]

Based on the condition of the bodies and their respective levels of algor and rigor, there is no question Binder died first, and that 8 a.m. was a reasonable time of death. Doak's body, on the other hand, suggested he had only been dead one to two hours at most when he was found by Woolams and Clarke, placing his time of death between 3 and 4 p.m. — a time when Alikomiak was in Woolams's custody.

While the physical evidence does not exclude Alikomiak as a potential suspect in the murder of Binder, it does indicate neither killing could have happened as he claimed in his statements. The story and the forensic evidence do not match.

If Alikomiak did not kill Doak or Binder, why did he confess to the crimes? Two answers warrant consideration. First, Alikomiak believed there were financial and social benefits to admitting guilt. Appearing tough was a necessity for Inuit males. Ethnographer Knud Rasmussen once claimed to have visited an Inuit village in which virtually every male had committed murder because of "temper, jealousy, the desire for a wife or vendetta."[23] Wood cited Rasmussen's experience in one of his reports, noting "it is the exception where a man is a weakling or has something wrong with him, that a man has not at least one killing to his credit. These people are always on the offensive.... These people hold life very cheaply."[24] In a culture that equated violence with masculinity and power, claiming to have killed two white men would have improved Alikomiak's standing in the band.

There were also widespread misperceptions among the Inuit regarding the RCMP. During his investigation in Kent Peninsula, Doak lamented: "None of the natives with whom I came into contact have any idea who or what the Police are or what they are doing in the country."[25] To the Inuit, the RCMP were simply "the rich men of the country," and any Indigenous person associated with the police would reap the rewards. HBC Fur Trade Commissioner A. Brabant noted the Inuit referred to "all the native prisoners taken by the RCMP as 'employees' or 'the people who are working for the police.'"[26] Because of the experiences of Oblate-priest killers Sinnisiak and Uluksuk, being arrested was seen as a fast-track to wealth, easy living, and a certain degree of prestige. Judge Dubuc believed that, for the Inuit, "being fed and housed by the Police ... is not only a reward, but an honour."[27]

Alikomiak took full advantage of the opportunities presented to him as a result of his arrest. Despite Wood's contention that the young Inuk would do anything to avoid going to Herschel Island, Alikomiak appeared to enjoy the experience. Court observers noted he laughed often and "at inappropriate times,"[28] leaving the prisoner's dock "grinning and uncomprehending."[29] Apparently, no one had explained that the experience would end with a hangman's noose.

The second answer to the question of why Alikomiak confessed is that he never did. Careful review of his statements reveal none of his initial comments were self-incriminating. Whenever he was asked what happened, Alikomiak's first response was to say nothing, even when those posing the question were Inuit. At the seal camp, Kunana "asked the accused why he killed the two white men, but got no reply."[30] Investigators interpreted those silences as admissions of guilt.

When the accused finally broke his silence, his utterances were typically innocuous, but those statements were consistently interpreted as nefarious by investigators. For example, in his final interview with Wood, Alikomiak said he wanted to go to the seal camp because "I knew Constable Woolams and Mr. Clarke of HBC were there" — a statement containing no overt threat. It is only after a relentless barrage of leading questions that a criminal motivation was ascribed: Alikomiak headed for the seal camp intent on killing all the remaining white men in the region.

Investigators heard what they wanted to hear even when Alikomiak said nothing at all. No translator was present as Alikomiak walked with Woolams and Clarke through the crime scene. Woolams could not speak the local Inuit language, so Alikomiak "made signs" to communicate. In recounting Binder's death, Alikomiak stood on a chair and mimed a rifle being fired. Woolams took that to mean Alikomiak was confessing to shooting Binder, but the Inuk could have been describing how he looked through the window and saw someone else shoot the trader. (It should also be noted that no one examined the window pane to determine the bullet's direction of travel. Investigators never ruled out the possibility that the bullet was fired into the barracks from the outside.)

The same pattern held true for the other Inuit witnesses. Police had to push in order to get the answers they wanted. When Ayalegak first encountered Alikomiak in Tree River, he recalled Alikomiak saying, "there is no white men here." Only after additional questioning did Ayalegak revise his statement, claiming Alikomiak said, "I killed them both."[31]

There is an underlying tension in every relationship between the colonizer and those colonized. The Inuit used the term *ilira* to describe the deference or subservience they showed to any white man in a position of power.[32] Unaccustomed to being interrogated by an aggressive authority figure, the reflexive Inuit response was to appease, telling the white man whatever he wanted to hear.

Alikomiak's so-called confessions were not false so much as they were manufactured by others. His edited, translated words were the only evidence the court heard, and every one of those words had passed through RCMP interpreter Cyril Uingnek, a man with his own motivations in this case.

Seventeen

Open to Interpretation

A failure to communicate aptly describes the relationship between the northern RCMP detachments and the local populace they served. The point was driven home during Alikomiak's murder trial when Wood introduced the accused's confession. When Howatt asked if Inspector Wood had "any knowledge of the Eskimo language," Wood replied: "just a jargon." Howatt then asked if Wood was able to understand Alikomiak as he confessed. Wood insisted he "could follow the trend of the story and the outstanding facts," estimating he grasped "about three-quarters of it." When Cory raised the issue on cross-examination, asking if Wood could work without a translator, the inspector finally conceded he could not.

Howatt then called that translator to the stand. One of the first steps police normally take in a murder investigation is to determine who was near the victim at the time of the killing. Witnesses consistently claimed Doak was alone in the barracks on the morning of April 1, making Alikomiak the only possible killer by process of elimination.

All of the RCMP officers were accounted for that morning — Bonshor and Stevenson were headed to Great Slave Lake with the mail while Woolams stood guard at the seal camp — but no one noted the locations of the detachment's Indigenous employees. Convicted murderers Sinnisiak and Uluksuk worked as the detachment's guides and dog handlers, but their whereabouts on the day in question were never ascertained.

There was also a strong possibility Doak was not in the barracks that morning. To supplement his meagre RCMP salary, the corporal aggressively hunted for fur and maintained a series of trap lines which he checked daily.[1] If Binder was shot at 8 a.m., as the condition of his body suggested, Doak may have been miles away with his sled dogs tending his traps. No RCMP report noted the location or condition of Doak's dog team on the day of the murder.

Tree River was an active hub in the community. Toletuk and Ayalegak had arrived shortly after sunrise to trade fur, but police learned this only because the two traders accompanied Alikomiak back to the seal camp. Short of anyone else self-reporting, investigators had no way of knowing who might have come to Tree River on April 1.

Certainly, Binder was not alone that morning. The trader shared his HBC quarters with Toktogan and their two small children. From the outset, Inspector Wood insisted Toktogan was "not implicated in any way with the murder of Binder,"[2] although he had no compelling evidence to support his contention. Local HBC employees claimed that, in marrying Binder, Toktogan's "lot in life is much improved and if one may judge by appearances — she appreciates it."[3] Wood's perception was that she had won a lottery of sorts and would have done nothing to threaten her windfall.

Toktogan's band saw things differently. In their view, Binder had stolen Toktogan from her husband and family, a punishable action under traditional Inuit law. Inuit scholars Aupilaarjuk et al. report that such punishments did not always come swiftly, nor was the right to retaliate reserved only for the injured party.[4] Despite the seeming air of calm, the Indigenous population had not forgotten or forgiven what Binder had done.

Losing Toktogan was strongly felt by the band because she was "quite good looking" and seemed "a very nice girl."[5] Her beauty and spirit turned Binder's head and she had not gone unnoticed by another. Cyril Uingnek was captivated by Toktogan, and the feeling was mutual. According to Cyril's testimony at trial, the pair began having an affair while she was still married to Ikialgagina, and the relationship continued when Toktogan moved to Tree River in 1920 to partner with Binder.[6]

On May 1, 1922 — exactly one month after Binder was killed — Cyril and Toktogan became man and wife.[7]

Even Thomas Cory recognized the timing was a little too convenient and questioned Cyril's ability to remain objective in his translations.

Tree River RCMP translator Cyril Uingnek, an Inuvialuit man from the Mackenzie Delta who was educated at a Church of England school near Great Slave Lake. Prior to working for the Mounties, Uingnek spent a year translating for Eldon Merritt, an Anglican missionary at St. Andrew's in Bernard Harbour.

With Cyril seated in the dock, Cory tried to raise the issue at trial, but Dubuc repeatedly dismissed any suggestion the translator had a conflict of interest.

Dubuc took the matter one step further. In the trial transcript sent to the Justice Department and governor general for review, Dubuc circled a reference to Toktogan as Binder's wife and in the margin wrote: "This title is a misnomer. Binder was unmarried. The woman — widow — kept house for Binder. She might as well be called the housekeeper." Dubuc knew Toktogan had a child by Binder — she testified to that effect in open court — but the judge had no patience for the entire line of questioning. Cory dropped his objections, Cyril was permitted to testify, and his translations were accepted into evidence.

Cyril's testimony revealed one final secret, a fact he had learned in the days before Binder and Doak were shot. Otto Binder was due to be transferred by the Hudson's Bay Company. Binder had told Cyril he would soon be "sent East," leaving the fate of Toktogan in question.[8] The transfer was likely only a rumour — Binder's HBC employment record contained no mention of any pending reassignment — but the prospect of losing his paramour gave Cyril Uingnek motive to act.[9]

To remove any whiff of scandal, Constable Woolams retook the stand and declared that everyone at Tree River was one big happy family and that Binder actually planned to "gift" Toktogan to Cyril when he went east.[10] Woolams then quickly redirected the jurors' attention back to Alikomiak's confession and the victims' devastating injuries.

Cyril's skill as a translator had been a point of contention long before the affair, the murders, or the trials. Doak had often complained he was not a "first-class interpreter"[11] and that Cyril had a tendency to be creative with his translations.[12] He also spoke a different dialect. The local bands were Inuinuait, whereas Cyril was Inuvialuit.[13] As a result, Cyril was "a little timid in dealing with the Copper Eskimo."[14]

Careful parsing of Cyril's translations reveals an alarming degree of congruity among witness statements.[15] Alikomiak claimed "his reason for killing Cpl. Doak was that he was frightened of him, and he killed Binder as he thought that if he saw Cpl. Doak's body he would most likely shoot him."[16] A virtually identical statement appeared in Cyril's translation of Toktogan's interview one week later.[17]

Such overt repetition raises red flags, as does the way the interviews were conducted. Toktogan, a key prosecution witness, was present during Alikomiak's third interrogation, a violation of protocols requiring witnesses to be questioned separately to prevent collusion, tampering, or intimidation.[18] There was no reason for her presence, beyond her role as the translator's new wife.

One final detail warrants serious consideration: Cyril Uingnek was at the Tree River detachment on April 1, 1922. His whereabouts went unaccounted for in the police reports, but witness statements recounted his movements throughout the day.

On April 1, Woolams sent Cyril with a packet of RCMP reports from the seal camp to the Tree River detachment. He left before dawn, hoping to catch Bonshor and Stevenson before they made the mail run to Great Slave Lake. Woolams had no way of knowing the constables had already departed, leaving Doak as the only officer in the barracks.[19] Cyril would have arrived at the camp well before Binder was shot at 8 a.m.

Cyril's actions and whereabouts from 6:30 a.m. to 1 p.m. were not recorded in any report. He was never asked to account for his time. The next mention of Cyril's activities came from Constable Woolams during his trial testimony. Woolams stated Cyril first told him there had been a shooting at around 1 p.m., shortly after Uingnek returned from delivering the mail to Tree River.

From this point on, problems with the timeline and recollection abound. Woolams's testimony contradicted his prior accounts, in which he first claimed to have learned of Doak and Binder's deaths at 3 p.m.[20] There was also debate as to who told Woolams about the killings. According to C.H. Clarke, Inspector Wood, and the two Indigenous traders, Toletuk and Ayalegak first broke the news at 3 p.m.[21] Woolams and Cyril both testified the news came from Cyril at 1 p.m.[22]

The disparity was significant because of what came next. Cyril immediately identified Alikomiak as the shooter. During the preliminary hearing, Cyril said he had learned of the killings when he crossed paths with Toletuk, Ayalegak, Alikomiak, and Toktogan while en route to the seal camp.[23] Upon reaching the camp, Cyril told Woolams "of the killing" and, on the constable's instructions, brought Alikomiak into custody.[24] All accounts agree Cyril delivered Alikomiak to Woolams at 3 p.m.

Cyril had found Alikomiak in Toletuk's igloo, situated a short distance from Woolams's snow house. By all accounts,[25] Alikomiak surrendered without any resistance, so why did it take two hours for Cyril to bring him to Woolams? One possibility was that Cyril used the time to convince Alikomiak to accept responsibility for the murders. Alikomiak would have been easily persuaded, given that his only point of reference was Sinnisiak and Uluksuk, who had profited handsomely from having shot two white priests.[26] Cyril, on the other hand, understood the role of the police and the real-life consequences of murder.

From that moment forward — through months of incarceration, numerous statements to police, and his testimony in court during Tatamigana's trial — Alikomiak's every word was translated by Cyril Uingnek.[27]

Once Alikomiak was in custody, Woolams needed his fellow officers' help with the investigation. He asked Cyril to overtake Bonshor and Stevenson on the trail to Great Slave Lake. Just after 3 p.m., Cyril took an RCMP dog team and rode out of the seal camp. He was once again alone and unaccounted for, and would remain so until he met up with Bonshor and Stevenson on April 3.

Woolams then asked C.H. Clarke to accompany him to Tree River. Woolams wanted an extra man to help control Alikomiak and he needed Clarke's dogs as they were "the only available team in camp."[28] Woolams, Clarke, and Alikomiak left the seal camp at roughly 3:15 p.m., arriving at Tree River two hours later.

If Corporal Doak was murdered mid-afternoon, as the degree of livor and algor mortis suggests, Cyril had a window of opportunity to commit the act. He had a head-start on Woolams and would have made better time travelling alone compared to three men struggling with a single sled and team.

As for why Cyril might have killed Doak, it was likely an unpremeditated act. Perhaps he roused a sleeping Doak, exhausted from a morning of fur trapping. Fearing for his own life, Cyril shot the corporal to evade capture.

Perhaps some hint rests in Doak's final words — "What is the matter with you?" — an utterance that makes more sense directed at Cyril than at Alikomiak. The only Inuk in Tree River capable of understanding Doak's dying words was Cyril Uingnek. Had Cyril inadvertently inserted a fact only he could have known into the supposed confession of the person he framed for murder?

Cyril Uingnek had motive and opportunity, but the police never considered him a suspect. The questions raised by his court testimony were left unchallenged. Too little evidence and too many unknowns remain to determine Cyril's culpability in the deaths of Doak or Binder, but his story proves a salient point: it is easy to make someone look guilty when you have complete control over the narrative.

Eighteen
Closing Arguments

Forensic science and alternative suspects meant nothing to Judge Dubuc as he shepherded his ground-breaking trial to a close. Alikomiak's guilt and the outcome of the proceedings were never in doubt. With both parties rested, the judge called for closing arguments.

Dubuc would later describe Cory's final summation as "emotional and so sentimental," noting that counsel had "displayed a skill of rare ability in his touching so forcibly the strings of the human heart on behalf of these poor people."

We cannot know what emotional plea Cory made on his clients' behalf. Court stenographer Richard S. Wild captured every syllable of Dubuc's epic seven-thousand-word summation, but he failed to record the closing arguments from either party — a violation of court procedure and the rules of law. The transcript simply reads: "Mr. Cory replied on behalf of the Defence."

A lone snippet of Cory's closing oration was committed to paper. He told jurors his clients should not be executed "since the uncivilized Eskimo are practically in the same condition as early Briton of 2,000 years ago," a rather obscure reference for a panel of rough-and-tumble northerners.[1]

Nothing survives of the Crown's closing argument, and Dubuc reserved judgment as to its emotional impact.

As Howatt reclaimed his seat, Dubuc offered his own summation to the court. He spoke eloquently, seemingly off the cuff. His delivery was soaring, his voice commanding — a stirring performance of questionable content. Dubuc began by stating there were "civilized and uncivilized portions" of Canada, the primitive sections populated by a single race of "unruled Eskimo" with "simple mentality."[2] His paternalistic view of "these Northern wards of ours"[3] had coloured his language throughout the trials, as he continually belittled "these uncivilized and unChristianized nomad tribes."

He admonished jurors "to uphold the superiority of the White race and show the benefits of Christianity to these less favoured people." His final instructions left little doubt as to the outcome he expected: "Our Government has not undertaken this expensive Judicial Expedition to have exhibited a mockery and travesty of justice before these primitive people." Scholars contend Dubuc's closing summation was so "graphic," "stirring" and unquestionably "biased" that "it would surely lead to a successful appeal for a new trial."[4]

Before releasing the jury to deliberate, Justice Dubuc directed some final thoughts to the gallery. The judge told the assembled Inuit of the glory of British justice, "which has been the envy of all other Nations," and the role it now played in this "no man's land." Dubuc insisted he had tried his very best and, if any legal mistakes were made, he was "not conscious of having done anything wrong morally, for there is a higher tribunal which will set me right." Whether Dubuc was referring to God or the Department of Justice was not clear.

The judge's instructions to the jury lasted almost two hours, but the panel deliberated just eighteen minutes before returning with a guilty verdict on both counts. Silence filled the court, broken only by Dubuc's proclamation that he would delay sentencing until a later date.

With death sentences looming, Dubuc's early decision to fraternize with Alikomiak and Tatamigana weighed heavily on his mind. Ethical violations aside, Dubuc's choice cost him the public's trust. As Alikomiak was taken from the courtroom after the verdict was rendered, he paused to hand Judge Dubuc a cigarette.[5] Such conviviality drew criticism. Reporters noted the convicted Inuit "treated the trial as a joke and, if freed, the law will be brought into contempt."[6] Indeed, Alikomiak "laughed so often during his trial" that protestors later argued he must be hanged "so as not to make a mockery of justice."[7]

Dubuc also paid a more personal price for his choice. Having spent time with the defendants, he struggled with the reality of condemning them to death. The judge even floated a number of alternatives to capital punishment, suggesting to the Secretary of State that the Criminal Code be amended to empower him "to sentence a criminal Eskimo to imprisonment on bread and water and inflict the lash."[8] Dubuc argued the lash held more power than the noose: "To be whipped is to be treated like a dog and is to them the greatest humiliation; such a sentence would be real punishment and one they could understand." His suggestions were met with silence.

Whatever affection Dubuc held for Alikomiak and Tatamigana, he understood what must come next: "I feel it my duty, although very painful to me, to recommend most respectfully, but most earnestly, that the Law follow its course."

On August 11, Judge Dubuc reconvened the court for the penalty phase. Following yet another lengthy statement on the splendour of Canadian jurisprudence, Dubuc called the convicted men to rise and stand before him. He solemnly decreed that Tatamigana was sentenced to hang by the neck until dead for his part in the shooting of Pugnana. In an equally stentorian tone, Dubuc condemned Alikomiak to the same fate for killing Pugnana, Doak, and Binder.

The date of those executions had long been a matter of debate. Inspector Wood wanted a speedy resolution, suggesting October 17.[9] The minister of justice had cautioned restraint, insisting Dubuc allow sufficient time for the verdicts to be reviewed in Ottawa before proceeding. Dubuc pleased no one by setting an execution date of December 7, arguing it was "easier to postpone than advance the date."[10]

Apropos of nothing, Dubuc then offered some life lessons to the jury. "You are just a handful of white men," the judge said, "and life would be more cheerful in every way if each one endeavoured to throw a mantle of Christian charity on the other's human weakness." Dubuc chastised the panel for "spreading false news, calumny and slander," adding, "these petty jealousies and stinging critiques make life miserable." Dubuc ended by stating that life on Herschel would be greatly improved if the government could see fit to install a wireless station.

With that and a final rap of his gavel, Justice Lucien Dubuc brought his unprecedented experiment in northern justice to a close.

Less than twelve hours later, the judicial party reassembled on the shore to board a launch, the first step in their protracted journey home to Edmonton. With his clients sitting on death row, Thomas Cory wanted off the god-forsaken rock. His mistrust of the Inuit had only grown during his time in the far North and he became increasingly paranoid.

Cory left the island with the rest of the judicial party, but trouble arose the moment the group landed in Aklavik. Cory wanted to part ways with the large entourage but was too frightened to complete the journey on his own. He approached Inspector Wood and demanded a personal police escort to see him safely back to Edmonton. Wood refused, telling Cory he was not in any danger nor could Wood spare the manpower. Cory sent word to his father, pleading with him to use his considerable influence to make Wood comply. Cory Senior placed a call to Cortlandt Starnes on his son's behalf. Shortly thereafter, Wood ordered a constable who was due for discharge to hold Cory's hand back to civilization.[11]

Once there, Cory gave a single post-conviction interview to the *Winnipeg Free Press* on November 1, 1923. He maintained his clients were guilty and the punishment was just.

........-----— — —-----........

Judge Dubuc's departure from Herschel was far less dramatic. Unlike Cory, the judge had relished his time on the island and was sad to leave. "We all had a very pleasant journey," he wrote to his superiors, "and we return with a greater knowledge of the resources and possibilities of our vast country."[12] In his missives south, Dubuc also revealed that he had delayed the sentencing hearing to the last possible moment because he wanted to ensure his sojourn in the Arctic would be an enjoyable one. He had held off delivering his "hanging speech" so as "not to cast a pall over the remainder of his stay on the island."[13]

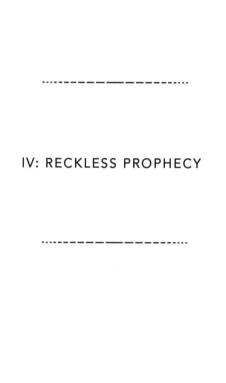

IV: RECKLESS PROPHECY

The verdict in all cases seemed to have met with the general approval of both the whites and the natives of the district.... If the sentence of the court is carried out, the Eskimo will henceforth understand that they must not take the law into their own hands.

— Judge Lucien Dubuc
Letter to Secretary of State, September 29, 1923

Nineteen

Men of Uncertain Age

Reverend James R. Lucas was having none of it. As the Anglican bishop of Mackenzie River, Lucas had ministered to and lived among the Inuit for years. He attended every moment of the trials and was mortified by the proceedings. Lucas voiced his outrage in three letters he posted to the Department of Justice and two western newspapers.[1]

Lucas's accounts exposed Ottawa's secret machinations. Contrary to the initial glowing media reports proclaiming the trials as masterpieces of Canadian justice,[2] Lucas painted the hearings as a travesty and farce. "It was painfully evident," wrote Lucas, "that the men were condemned before [the judicial party] left Edmonton."

The bishop took Dubuc, the RCMP, and the Justice Department to task for the "unwanted spectacle [of] a judge, hangman and gallows travelling together to Herschel Island." He was particularly appalled that the graves for Alikomiak and Tatamigana were dug one week before the trial took place.

Lucas also laid bare Binder's troubles with the Indigenous community. He placed the responsibility for the Kent Peninsula massacre squarely at Binder's feet, as well as culpability for his own death and that of Doak. The root cause of the bloodshed, Lucas argued, "can be traced back to the actions of [Binder] in wresting an Eskimo woman from an Eskimo man."

Lucas ended his letters with an ominous prediction: "the execution of these two men will jeopardize the lives of white men … living amongst the tribes of Eskimos."

Cortlandt Starnes, ever vigilant of public opinion, was in equal measure outraged and frightened by Lucas's exposé. Parsing the bishop's comments, Starnes recognized one rumour he could quash. The commissioner asked Thomas P. O'Kelly, captain of the HBC steamship *Kindersley*, whether there was any truth to the notion that "the feud among the Eskimo was apparently caused by the stealing of a woman, and that the [massacre] was probably a consequence of this."[3] O'Kelly assured him Binder's relationship "had no connection whatever with any of the killings." Starnes passed the captain's assurances to the Justice Department "as it may be useful to have," adding it might not be "a bad idea if it was given to the press in some way or another."

The fallacy of a monolithic North and its generic "Eskimo" inhabitants was not the only widely held misperception among whites at the time. Clergymen in the North believed "Eskimos are children of the wild who remain children always." The stereotype would become a constant drumbeat in the growing number of petitions and protests calling for Ottawa to commute the death sentences of Alikomiak and Tatamigana. Dr. Wilfred Grenfell, a medical missionary who worked among the Inuit, argued: "To hang an Eskimo for murder is the same as hanging a little child.… The Eskimos are an extraordinarily intelligent people … but they are totally ignorant of law and the consequences of its violation. Ethically, the Eskimo is just a child of seven years. You would not hang a child of seven years, would you?"[4]

The question shifted from hyperbole to pressing reality when Reverend Lucas delivered one final revelation: Alikomiak was actually still a child.

In his letters south, Lucas revealed Alikomiak was at most sixteen years old, making him a legal minor. The public response was immediate and vociferous, prompting scores of politicians, legal notables, and everyday citizens to write the minister of justice pleading for a stay of execution.[5]

The revelation also unleashed some fevered scrambling in Ottawa. Cortlandt Starnes wrote the Department of Justice, saying: "As you know, Eskimos keep no track of their ages, and it is therefore only by their

Reverend James R. Lucas, Anglican bishop of Mackenzie River, photographed in Aklavik in 1922. Lucas was born on August 20, 1867, in Brighton, England, and studied at CMS College in Islington before immigrating to Canada in 1891. He was appointed the region's bishop in 1912.

appearance and the knowledge of other people that an estimate can be made."[6] The commissioner knocked back Lucas's allegation with a statement from Peter Norberg, the HBC's manager in Kent Peninsula. Norberg claimed, "It is extremely difficult to estimate his age but I would say he was about 19." Norberg added he "has known this boy six years and that he looks the same now as when he first saw him."[7]

Starnes slipped that information to a reporter at the *Ottawa Morning Journal*. The paper published a prominent rebuttal to Lucas's accusation, claiming the public had been "misled by erroneous reports of facts."[8] The *Journal* took a swipe at its big city rivals, dismissing "popular indignation" and Toronto media reports that Alikomiak was sixteen when those who knew Alikomiak personally said he was between twenty and twenty-five.

Alikomiak, photographed by journalist Miriam Green Ellis during her trip to Aklavik, June 1922. Ellis included a hand-painted version of the image in her "Magic Lantern" lecture when she returned south, giving the public their first glimpse of the accused Inuit. The photo was also widely reproduced in the press, reigniting speculation as to Alikomiak's real age.

Judge Lucien Dubuc took this photograph of Alikomiak as both awaited the sentencing phase of the trial. Herschel Island, late July/early August 1923. Dubuc remained noticeably silent on the question of Alikomiak's age during the public furor that erupted in the fall of 1923.

One month later, Starnes privately acknowledged Alikomiak was likely sixteen, conceding it "would be most unusual to carry out the capital sentence on a boy of that age."[9]

Neither the RCMP nor the Justice Department could rightfully claim ignorance. Inspector Wood had instantly recognized Alikomiak's age would be an issue. In his first report, Wood noted the accused looked extremely young. He identified Peter Norberg as "the only witness as to the approximate age of the prisoner," making him "a necessary witness."[10] Norberg later made the long journey to Herschel Island to testify, but was never called to the stand.

The Inuit had no relationship with the Gregorian calendar. During the trial, Cory asked Tatamigana how old Alikomiak might be. Tatamigana did not know, saying only that he knew himself to be older. When asked his own age, Tatamigana had no idea.

Even Alikomiak could not resolve the debate. When pressed repeatedly he would not hazard to guess, telling police during his interrogations: "I do not know how old I am." During his second grilling, Alikomiak provided a lone point of reference when he stated he had "hunted for the first time a year ago this winter and could not hunt before that because I had no rifle or bow or arrows." Ethnographer Knud Rasmussen's studies of the Copper Inuit indicate a boy's first hunt occurred at puberty, suggesting Alikomiak was in his early teens when Doak and Binder were shot.[11] Modern Indigenous researchers fix the developmental marker as young as seven.[12] All agree no band could afford to sustain a healthy male in his early to mid-twenties who was not hunting and contributing to the band's welfare.

Alikomiak's unmarried status also challenges the RCMP estimate. Most Inuit were married at a young age, with men taking a bride shortly after reaching puberty. Before an Inuk could marry, he had to have killed his first caribou or adult seal, a milestone Alikomiak had yet to reach.[13]

Alikomiak's tender age had rendered him immune within his own band from any consequences in the killing of Pugnana. Traditional Inuit justice was forgiving of juveniles who kill. As one modern elder has noted, "there was no reason to deal with it."[14]

Leniency toward juvenile offenders was the one issue on which Canadian and Inuit laws agreed. In 1908, the Canadian legislature passed the Juvenile

Delinquents Act, decreeing "youthful offenders should not be classed or dealt with as ordinary criminals." The law applied to and expressly protected anyone sixteen years of age or less.[15]

The act also declared the Juvenile Court had "exclusive jurisdiction" over cases involving minors. Alikomiak's age was not simply another Ottawa PR disaster or a cause célèbre for Toronto liberals. If Alikomiak truly was sixteen, Judge Dubuc's court had no authority to try his case.

Twenty

Meanwhile, South of Sixty ...

Reverend Lucas's depiction of anxious hangmen, pre-tied nooses, and waiting graves had stoked the ire of humanists and drawn cheers from those who believed that "English rule over wild, untutored races" was both necessary and as God intended.[1] Days after his letters to the editor appeared, seven petitions began circulating in Toronto demanding a stay of execution.[2] The hew and cry took its toll on the saga's key players.

Justice Dubuc was accustomed to a smooth ride, having somehow crafted a life of adventure curiously devoid of struggle. There had been one brief bout of turbulence in 1906 when Dubuc first sought public office. He had won a seat in the Alberta legislature as an independent, but the province overturned the result because of "significant irregularities" during polling, leading some to question whether the vote was held at all.[3] Since then, Dubuc had escaped all public criticism or professional censure. When he stepped off the train in Edmonton on September 21, 1923, still flush from overseeing the "first Canadian court held in the regions of the Polar Sea," the judge was stunned when his foot landed in a steaming pile of condemnation and scorn.[4]

Mrs. E. Maitland of Plummer, Ontario, captured the prevailing sentiment:

> Although a woman, I am not one who favours the abolition
> of the death penalty ... but it seems not unreasonable to

sympathize with these ignorant, primitive people, standing confused and bewildered in one of our law courts, and so simple-minded and remote from the subtleties of "civilized" law proceedings that they told a straight-forward tale, which practically convicted themselves.[5]

Little of the public vitriol was thrown directly at Dubuc, but he considered his court a reflection of his character. He took the rebukes personally, adopting a defensive stance. Like Starnes, Dubuc felt compelled to swing at every pitch, attempting to silence all critics and run damage control in the press. He wrote letters to colleagues and the newspapers, scribbled frantic notes in the margins of court documents, and fired off costly telegrams of astonishing length — bursting at the margins and extending over many pages — justifying his every decision.[6] Dubuc's quixotic fight proved futile as negative media coverage of the case went national, then spread south and across the Atlantic.[7]

RCMP commanders in the North dismissed most of the articles as "rot," but Cortlandt Starnes was not amused. He collected disparaging news clippings and began silencing the critics through whatever means necessary.[8] Starnes was particularly irked by a piece in the Toronto *Globe* entitled "The Doomed Eskimos," written by A.E. McFarlane. The op-ed was highly unflattering to the RCMP and DOJ, and made very specific allegations of court misconduct.

In a confidential letter Starnes ordered H.M. Newson to "make discrete [*sic*] inquiries regarding A. McFarlane, the person who has been writing so energetically about the Eskimos." Starnes's spies had told him McFarlane was spending time in Ottawa regarding "that agitation," and the commissioner wanted to know why.[9] Newson told Starnes, "Coronal Hamilton has already asked about McFarlane" but Newson had yet to find "anything of interest."[10] Newson then interviewed the editor of the *Globe*, Mr. Hammond, who told him McFarlane was a professional writer with several novels and magazine articles to his credit. McFarlane had a brother-in-law living in the North who appeared to be the source of his information.[11] At the end of the interview, Mr. Hammond requested that "his name be kept out of anything which may transpire."

Starnes continued his surveillance of McFarlane but, by mid-November, Newson admitted the campaign to silence McFarlane had led nowhere.[12] The matter was quietly dropped.

It is at this point that my investigation of this case takes a curious turn. All of the documentation generated by the RCMP and the Department of Justice regarding the murders of Doak and Binder, and the subsequent trials, is currently stored at the national archives in Ottawa. All files are open to the public, save one: RG 85, vol 607, 2580, 1923-1926, which is "restricted by law." The file contains Cortlandt Starnes's private communications regarding the executions of Alikomiak and Tatamigana. After several written requests, I was granted access to the file in May 2017. It was soon apparent why the RCMP wanted the file to remain off limits.

Clearly, Reverend Lucas's public castigation had stuck in the commissioner's craw. Starnes vented his rage by throwing his subordinates under whatever vehicle was most convenient: "It is not enough that the man [Gill] should have given himself away before leaving Edmonton, and that the party had to gossip all over the place about it, but I cannot understand that Wood should have been fool enough to have had the gallows erected and graves dug before the sentence was approved."[13] Starnes also acknowledged the magnitude of the public relations disaster: "If it has been done as [Lucas] stated, we would be in a most ridiculous position and Wood has shown a great lack of judgment."[14] Having issued the orders regarding the hangman, Starnes's final thought was for himself: "I dare not deny anything. I can only keep my mouth shut."

The commissioner's silence did not last long. He began to wonder whether Lucas was mistaken. Starnes wrote to Wood's supervisor in Edmonton, clinging desperately to a last sliver of hope: "Surely Inspector Wood did not go so far as to dig the graves and erect the scaffold at such an early date. Please wire me in cipher as early as possible."[15]

The response was clipped and crushing. Commander James Ritchie telegrammed: "Unfortunately [the] report about scaffolding is true."[16] Inspector Wood staunchly defended his decision: "It is most regrettable that any such information should be published, however, I believe I was justified in having the scaffold built while I had the men there to do it."[17] What Wood could not explain was how Lucas knew about the gallows: "The work was done behind closed doors and the place kept locked so that outsiders could only have surmised that the scaffold was built, certainly Bishop Lucas never saw it."

The good news, if Starnes strained to see it, was the graves. Based on messages relayed from Wood to Edmonton to Ottawa, Starnes informed the

Justice Department[18] that the graves "referred to in the press" were in fact dug to hold the relocated remains of Sergeant Selig, a Mountie who died on Herschel Island in 1911 but was interred in the Whalers burying grounds.[19] Realizing this might explain one grave but not two, Starnes suggested the other was for Doak's remains, slated to be exhumed from Tree River and brought to Herschel Island. Starnes claimed Bishop Lucas knew this before he sent his toxic letters south. The commissioner assured the justice minister, "there is not foundation in the rumour that the graves were dug for the condemned Eskimos before the trial took place."[20]

Starnes took the matter one step further by issuing an immediate press release declaring the graves "were dug for the reinterment [*sic*] of the victims."[21] Starnes's account was not accurate, but it seemed plausible. Few papers ran the notice, preferring to stick with Lucas's version of events.

Confidential documents buried in the restricted archival case file contradict Starnes's assertion that one of the graves was for Doak.[22] By the time the commissioner issued his press release, the RCMP had already authorized the purchase of an eighty-five-dollar marble headstone for Doak's grave in Tree River, but only after first considering a much cheaper wooden memorial.[23]

The graves of Corporal William Doak and Otto Binder near the Tree River detachment in the Northwest Territories, photographed by a tourist, circa 1923.

As for relocating Doak's remains, the issue had become a sore subject at headquarters. One year after Doak's death, his brother sent a formal request to the RCMP asking that the remains be moved to the Regimental Cemetery on Herschel Island.[24] The request bounced between detachments as inquiries were made. A petition to the HBC to transport the body aboard their supply ship was emphatically refused "on the grounds that there were no facilities on the boat for the proper preservation of the body."[25] Weeks before Starnes issued his press release, he had already decided Doak's grave would remain in Tree River.

Equally damning was a confidential letter from Inspector Wood detailing the creation of Alikomiak and Tatamigana's graves: "Const. Myhill and McDonald worked for a few hours one night but had to abandon the work on account of water. No one at Herschel Isl. knows of this even at present outside our own men. By no possible means could anyone connect the grave dug in July as being for the reception of condemned prisoners."[26]

Starnes continued tilting at windmills and counterpunching in the media, but to no avail. The public outcry had grown too strong, and soon the RCMP commissioner was not the only one with an "Eskimo" problem.

The question of jurisdiction resurfaced with a vengeance. At the time, Canada had no official policy regarding the northern Indigenous people. To fill the void, William Cory, as minister of the Northwest Territories, declared the "Eskimos" to be his "wards," thereby giving him responsibility for their punishment.[27] Dr. Duncan Campbell Scott simultaneously announced his intention to amend the Indian Act to bring the Inuit under his purview. Scott won in the end, although it took a landmark ruling by the Supreme Court of Canada in 1939 to determine that "Eskimos were Indians," temporarily bringing the northern First Nations under the jurisdiction of the Indian Act.[28]

Such inter-departmental bickering carried no weight on Herschel Island, where the gallows and graves awaited the condemned Inuit.

Twenty-One

Stunt Man

As officials squabbled over ownership of the Inuit, a new hero rose to claim the spotlight: Sergeant Hubert George Thorne. The exploits of Sergeant Thorne would be Cortlandt Starnes's media masterstroke — a way to shift the national conversation and restore the reputation of his beleaguered force.

At age thirty-eight, Thorne was a recruiting-poster Mountie, blessed with chiseled good looks and broad shoulders seemingly built to wear the red serge. He was also no stranger to the North, having served as a court escort during the LeBeau trial in 1921.[1] Starnes had hand-picked Thorne for a crucial assignment.

Canadian law required the governor general to sign off on all capital punishment verdicts. On October 8, 1923, after much input from the justice minister, Lord Byng completed his review of the case. He declared he was "unable to order any interference with the sentence," and commanded the RCMP to "proceed with the executions" as scheduled on December 7.[2]

Starnes ordered Thorne to hand-deliver the death warrants, a task requiring a gruelling five-thousand-mile trek from Vancouver to Herschel Island.[3] It would be a race against time and a test of man against the elements. It was also pure theatre. The much-heralded death warrants were nothing more than a single short telegram Starnes had sent to the RCMP commander of Vancouver, who in turn gave it to Thorne to pass on to Inspector Wood.[4]

THROUGH NORTH'S WHITE WASTE UNDER THE SHIMMERING AURORA SPEEDS MESSENGER OF DEATH

Doom Pronounced by Canadian Law Will Be Fulfilled When Lone Police Officer Reaches Most Northerly Post, Where Law's Representatives Await His Coming to Proceed to Execution of Two Eskimos Convicted of Murder in Course of Blood Feud

TWO MEN WILL DIE AT END OF JOURNEY, AND CANADA'S RULE WILL BE VINDICATED

Vancouver, Oct. 16.—"I'll be back in January. Goodbye!" casually remarked Sergeant Hubert Thorne of that famous Canadian frontier force, the Royal Canadian Mounted It is this message of death which Thorne carries with him in his dash through the trackless wastes of snow and ice from Fort Yukon to Herschel Island. Already, the wild geese honk their way south to the Ever-

Sergeant Hubert George Thorne graced the pages of the Toronto *Globe*, October 18, 1923. Thorne was born on May 13, 1884, in Hampshire, England. Craving adventure, he emigrated to Canada and joined the North-West Mounted Police. Although he never served in the active military, he did apply to the Canadian Overseas Expeditionary Force in 1918, one year after marrying his Nova Scotia–born wife, Alvah Louis Lewis.

Starnes's mind was clearly on optics rather than expedience. Had he wanted to ensure the message arrived on Herschel in a timely manner, he could have sent the telegram directly to Fort Yukon and had a member of that detachment carry it north, shaving almost four thousand miles off the roundtrip journey.

Instead, Starnes ordered Thorne to travel from his home detachment in Edmonton to Vancouver to begin his noble quest, all to collect a telegram capable of going wherever it was sent. Thorne could have saved time and money by heading north from Edmonton, but Starnes wanted him in the media-rich environment of Vancouver, with its easy access to the neighbouring U.S. markets. The arrangement suited Thorne; before he left Vancouver, "there were several things [he] wanted to get; amongst them, an eiderdown robe."[5]

The media obsessed over Thorne's every step with fawning front-page coverage. To great fanfare he departed Vancouver for Seattle on October 11, the first leg of a round-trip odyssey that would ultimately take seventy-five days and cover over 7,493 miles, 1,025 of those by dogsled.[6]

Thorne sent regular dispatches while en route. Starnes gleefully shared the telegrams with the press, but stopped once Thorne reached Alaska. A bout of unseasonably warm weather had brought Thorne's quest to a standstill:

"Thermometers fifty six above here this morning. No signs snow or rivers closing. No boats or stages." Acknowledging his rapidly diminishing options, Thorne asked Starnes to delay the executions: "Respectfully request date reset to December twenty eight as cannot make Herschel by December seventh."[7]

Starnes, too, had limited options. Once Thorne left Fort Yukon — the northernmost telegraph station on his route[8] — there could be no "eleventh hour" reprieve and no further communication. On November 14, 1923, the commissioner reluctantly postponed the executions until February 1, 1924.[9] Starnes accepted no responsibility, citing unexpected weather delays for Thorne's inability to reach Herschel Island in time. Starnes could not afford any further mistakes, and his final message sent to Fort Yukon warned the sergeant to "take great care to see that all necessary formalities required by law are carried out prior to, during and after executions."[10]

Thorne finally set foot on Herschel Island on the evening of December 6, 1923, less than six hours before the original scheduled time of execution.[11] He handed the "death warrant" telegram to Inspector Wood, unpacked his eiderdown robe, and settled in for fifty-six cold, dark days until the executions could be carried out.

Inspector Wood was glad for the extra manpower. Wood feared an Inuit revolt as the executions neared, telling his superiors: "They are giving no trouble so far but I would rather [be careful] then have to look forward to another performance next time."[12] Wood, too, could only sit and wait. Thanks to Starnes's prescient manoeuvres, the gallows had stood ready for almost seven months.

·························— — — ——— — — — —·············

As January waned, all eyes in the south turned toward Herschel Island. The press was again filled with debates on the evils and benefits of capital punishment, along with a few last-ditch appeals to reason.

The perpetual night of an Arctic winter lent the hangings an appropriate air, captured in blazingly purple prose by the London tabloid *News of the World*: "The execution took place with the lights of the Aurora Borealis illuminating the horizon. Silhouetted against the pink slashed sky, the frowning scaffold reared its ugly platform amid the pure white scape of a grandeur that nature rarely excels."[13] The report was all the more remarkable because it was published more than two weeks before the actual executions.

Twenty-Two

The Eternal Hunting Grounds

On the last day of their lives, Alikomiak and Tatamigana had no idea what was to come. They started the morning of January 31, 1924, as usual: fixing salmon nets for the island's villagers. Using Cyril as a go-between, Wood finally told the condemned men they were to be hanged the next morning. According to local Inuit observers, "young Alikomiak received the news with a smile."[1] Tatamigana "felt as if he were choking and asked for a glass of water." After draining his cup and a moment of quiet reflection, he stated that "he too was ready to meet his fate." The prisoners then returned to their nets, content to spend the remainder of their time on earth smoking and chatting amiably with their captors.

Meanwhile, Special Constable Gill slunk back to the island from Aklavik to survey his previous handiwork. The gallows was brutally simple: a log crossbar held aloft by two inverted-V uprights with some supplemental bracing. Two fixed-rope nooses hung from the crossbar. There was no long-drop trapdoor to break the prisoners' necks; the system relied solely on strangulation. A small crate, fashioned from the wooden box used to transport the ropes, was placed at the base of each noose. When the time came, the crates would be pulled out from under the condemned men, leaving them to slowly suffocate.

At 3:25 a.m. on February 1, Alikomiak was escorted from his cell to the shed where the gallows loomed.[2] He "appeared to be in high spirits," shaking hands with the few witnesses present.[3] Before he entered the former bone shed, he stopped to hand Mrs. Wood a small ivory carving, "a sign that [he] bore no malice towards the police."[4] Alikomiak even paused to offer Gill a cigarette.[5]

He was helped up onto his wooden crate as Gill fastened the noose around his neck. No hood or blindfold was used. Wood repeated Dubuc's sentencing statement, then Gill pulled the crate from beneath Alikomiak's feet. The young Inuk struggled, his body flailing as he fought for air. His death throes continued for fourteen minutes before he was declared dead.

Tatamigana met a similar fate at 3:55 a.m. He was pronounced dead nine minutes later by Dr. Doyle.

The only witnesses were Reverend Geddes of Shingle Point; Dr. Doyle; Inspector Wood; and his local constable, Corporal J.P. Pennefather.[6] Sergeant Thorne and a local HBC trader named A.A. Carroll were recruited as coroner's witnesses.[7] The hangings were intended to send a message to the Inuit, yet Wood was careful to ensure none were present that morning.

The inspector would later wish he had included Cyril Uingnek among the witnesses. Tradition dictated that prisoners be asked if they have any final words, and Wood posed the question to Alikomiak. Accounts differ as to what happened next. Wood claimed the boy "made no statement, was quite composed and gave no trouble whatsoever."[8] Coroner's jurymen Carroll and Thorne later told reporters Alikomiak had spoken for several minutes, ranting that the police hated the Inuit[9] and "had long been enemies of his people."[10] With no translator present, neither version seems entirely credible.

No autopsies had been performed on any of the murder victims, yet protocol demanded a physician certify the deaths of all executed prisoners. Since doctors were thin on the ground, Doyle was once again called to give his expertise. After a cursory examination, Doyle declared "Tatamigana was dead."[11] He drew the same conclusion regarding Alikomiak, adding "Death was due to fracture of the upper cervical vertebrae."[12] Doyle, Thorne, and Carroll then signed the necessary forms.

Gill's pretrial preparations included fashioning a pair of "rough coffins." The bodies were taken to the burying grounds and put on stages, where they remained until spring. Wood closed his final terse report by noting that neither condemned man had any property or personal effects "except for his clothing. CASE CONCLUDED."[13]

Word of the hangings did not reach the outside world until March 8, 1924. Thorne's telegraphed prose captured the moment for posterity:

"Prisoners Alikomiak and Tatamigana executed three fifty five morning February first STOP Everything satisfactory STOP."[14]

In the weeks following, it seemed everyone had an opinion. One of the loudest belonged to the nation's official executioner, Arthur Ellis. Ellis's services were not needed on Herschel Island and, while the slight clearly still rankled Ellis, his lack of participation did not prevent him from holding a press conference to discuss the hangings at length. Ellis had harsh words for his rival Fred A. Hill, a man Ellis dismissed as a rank amateur. "The Eskimo is just as much entitled to a decent hanging as a white man," Ellis told the press gaggle.[15]

Knud Rasmussen also weighed in. He estimated the cost of the trial and executions to be between $50,00 and $75,000,[16] later revising the figure to $100,000.[17] The lower end of Rasmussen's estimates appears reasonable. Although far from a comprehensive list, a total of all available invoices in the archives amounts to just under $25,000. Long before the trials began, the cost of the case had "exhausted" the RCMP's yearly budget for the region.[18]

In the decades since, scholars have argued the trials were a "sham" conducted solely to send a message, leaving many to wonder: "For whom was the show put on and to whom was the message directed?"[19] Debate also raged as to whether the case was effective as a deterrent. Legal scholar Sidney Harring noted that, following the deaths of Alikomiak and Tatamigana, "no more white men were killed by Inuit in the Arctic," although he credited this to "whites becoming more careful in their dealings with Inuit."[20] Other scholars contend the hangings did little to curb violence.[21]

The message also failed to land with its intended audience. Knud Rasmussen interviewed several members of Alikomiak and Tatamigana's band after the executions and reported that "all that great show of judges, jurymen and witnesses made no particular impression on them."[22]

The long-range impact of the trials and executions on the Inuit was far greater and more tangible. The proceedings set a crucial precedent, establishing Canadian rule of law over the northern Indigenous Peoples. Canada finally had a legally binding claim to the North and its inhabitants, solidifying the nation's governance of the land and its resources. Traditional Inuit law was usurped by the Canadian judicial system, which routinely imposed the Western notions of justice first espoused by Dubuc on Herschel Island. Dubuc's court became the status quo, defining the contentious relationship between the Inuit and the Canadian government for decades.

Unbowed, the Inuit fought to reclaim their autonomy. On April 1, 1999 — seventy-seven years to the day after Doak and Binder were killed — the map of Canada changed for the first time in fifty years. The Northwest Territories were divided in two, creating a new territory known as Nunavut — "our land" in the Inuktitut language. Nunavut is populated and largely governed by the Inuit, effectively returning control of the local courts back to the Indigenous people. While the Criminal Code of Canada still applies, the Inuit can now form a true jury of peers, and administer justice according to their beliefs and traditions.[23]

The final lingering vestiges of Dubuc's court were undone in 2009 with the Circumpolar Inuit Declaration of Sovereignty in the Arctic, which promotes autonomous rule to all Inuit living within the Arctic Circle.[24]

The sad saga of Alikomiak and Tatamigana would claim one final victim. During his fifth Thule expedition in 1924, Knud Rasmussen learned of the recent suicide of the father of one of the condemned Inuit.[25] Band members claimed the man killed himself when he realized his son would "undertake the long journey to the eternal hunting grounds." Local custom required someone to greet and guide all spirits passing over to the grounds.

Volunteering to be his son's guide proved harder than expected. The father first shot himself in the chest. When that failed, he tried stabbing himself in the heart. Still alive and increasingly desperate, the man took a knife to his throat, severing his carotid artery.[26] His body was buried according to custom — open to the air, covered only with some animal hides and a few blocks of ice. The timing of the suicide was not reported; there is no way to know whether the father greeted his son in the eternal hunting ground or if the son served as his father's guide.

To this day, Corporal William Doak and trader Otto Binder rest on an isolated plain tended by the Kugluktuk RCMP detachment. Their well-kept graves are bound by a white chain link fence, forever united by their tragic ends. Alikomiak and Tatamigana are buried side by side on a barren stretch of Herschel Island. Their graves are unmarked, invisible to passersby. Two young men reduced to a single violent footnote, forever united by the dubious distinction of being the only Inuit ever executed in Canada.[27]

Acknowledgements

Special thanks to Dr. Louis-Jacques Dorais, professor emeritus of anthropology at Laval University; Dr. Murielle Nagy, consultant in anthropology and archaeology; and Dr. André Bourcier, linguist at the Yukon Native Language Centre for their invaluable assistance with issues relating to the Inuit language and translations.

Thanks to Alex Somerville, executive director of the Dawson City Museum, for opening up the archives even though the museum was closed for the winter; and to Sue Parsons, collections manager, and Jody Beaumont of the Tr'ondëk Hwëch'in Han Nation for helping to solve the mystery of the "Han Boy." I am grateful to Shannon Olson and Brenda Berezan of the Yukon Archives; Linda Quirk of the Bruce Peel Special Collections at the University of Alberta; Adria Lund at the Glenbow Museum; Dr. Morgan Swan at the Rauner Special Collections Library at Dartmouth University; Anja Reimer, Museumsleder, Ilulissat City Museum; and Katherine Epp of the Provincial Archives of Alberta, for their assistance in locating and reproducing photographs.

I am indebted to Samantha Booth at the Hudson's Bay Company Archive at the Provincial Archives of Manitoba for helping me find materials relating to Otto Binder. Special thanks also to Alison Pier, Steve Irwin, Patrick Osborne, Brianne Boucher, and Michel Brideau at Library and

Archives Canada in Ottawa for accommodating my research requests and granting permission to view material previously restricted by law.

Finally, sincere thanks to the staff at Dundurn Press and my agent, Carolyn Swayze.

This book was researched and written during my time as writer-in-residence at Berton House in Dawson City, Yukon. It would not have been possible without the support of the Writer's Trust of Canada, the Canada Council for the Arts, the Berton family, and the people of Dawson City. My heartfelt thanks to you all for one of the greatest experiences of my life.

Notes

Prologue

1. Statement of Peter Norberg, HBC Manager, quoted in a report by Stuart Wood, July 2, 1922. RG 18, vol 3293, 1922-HQ-681-G-1, vol 1. Library and Archives Canada (hereafter LAC).
2. Miriam Green Ellis, "Eskimo Boy Who Shot Mountie," *Winnipeg Free Press*, November 18, 1922.
3. Alikomiak's statement at his preliminary hearing, April 17, 1923. RG 13 C-1, vol 1526, "Alikomiak," vol 1, Part 1. LAC.
4. Explorer Knud Rasmussen travelled to Kent Peninsula and interviewed contemporaries of both Alikomiak and Corporal Doak and was told by both sides the two men "could not speak to one another" (*Intellectual Culture of the Copper Eskimo: Report of the Fifth Thule Expedition, 1921– 1924*, vol 9 [Copenhagen: Gyldendalske Boghandel, 1932], 63).

Chapter One: Pristine Wasteland

1. Details of the region's history and quotes from Donald Prince, *The Inuit and Their Land: The Story of Nunavut* (Toronto: James Lorimer and Company, 1992), 29–38.

Chapter Two: The Mounties and "These People"

1. Ken S. Coates and William R. Morrison, "'To Make These Tribes Understand': The Trial of Alikomiak and Tatamigana," in *Strange Things Done: Murder in Yukon History* (Montreal: McGill-Queen's University Press, 2004), 99. Even those who lived and worked in the Arctic often failed to recognize the distinct bands, each with their own dialects, customs, and culture.

2. Robert J. Christopher, *Robert and Frances Flaherty: A Documentary Life, 1883–1922* (Montreal: McGill-Queen's University Press, 2005), 387–88. See also Erik Barnouw, *Documentary: A History of Non-Fiction Film* (Oxford: Oxford University Press, 1993), 33–36 and 47–48.

3. Edward Butts, "North-West Mounted Police," *The Canadian Encyclopedia*, www.thecanadianencyclopedia.ca/en/article/north-west-mounted-police.

4. Quoted in Philip H. Godsell, *They Got Their Man: On Patrol with the Northwest Mounted Police* (Toronto: Ryerson Press, 1932), 182.

5. Sidney L. Harring, "The Rich Men of the Country: Canadian Law in the Land of the Copper Inuit, 1914–1930," *Ottawa Law Review* 21, no. 1 (1989) 8–9. Lisa Beiler examined the claims of infanticide and found the practice to be extremely rare. To curb what they perceived as a rampant problem, the RCMP began issuing "baby bonuses" to the local people to dissuade them from killing their own children ("Alikomiak and Tatamigana: Justice and Injustice in the Canadian Arctic," MA Thesis, University of Waterloo, 2016: 37).

6. Knud Rasmussen, *Across Arctic America: Narrative of the Fifth Thule Expedition* (New York: Greenwood Press, 1927), 303.

7. Miriam Green Ellis, "Eskimo Boy Who Shot Mountie," *Winnipeg Free Press*, November 18, 1922.

8. RCMP Service Record for William A. Doak, 1905–1921. RG 18-G, vol 3466, file 4396. LAC.

9. "History of the RCMP," Royal Canadian Mountain Police, rcmp-grc.ca/en/history-rcmp. The new force scrambled to accommodate the change, including purchasing rubber stamps for their remote detachments to modify existing letterhead and documents. The stamp blocked out "North West," embossing "Canadian" in its place (see, for example, a

memo from R.S. Knight to C. Starnes, July 26, 1922, R196-158-9-E, 1905–1921. RG 18-G, vol 3466, file 4396. LAC).

10. RCMP Service Record for William A. Doak.

11. Doak's personal effects included four pipes and his final purchases from the company store included five hundred cigarettes, fifteen pounds of pipe tobacco, seven pounds of chewing tobacco and other smoking related items (RCMP Service Record for William A. Doak).

12. Letter from Lucien Dubuc to the Department of the Secretary of State, September 29, 1923. RG 13 C-1, vol 1526, vol 1, Part 1, CC207, No. 24861. LAC. Although Dubuc presented the translation as literal, he was technically incorrect as the word "police" had no direct translation in the local Inuit dialect. Dubuc's contention stemmed from accounts of prior interactions between the police and the local bands. When asked what the police were, the Inuit replied, "The rich men of the country."

13. RCMP Service Record for Corporal William Andrew Doak, Registration number 4396. RG 18-G, vol 3466, file 4396. LAC. Doak's salary was low even by the standards of the day. In 1921, the average Canadian school teacher earned $1,395/year (male teachers, that is; their female colleagues earned just $818 [R.D. Gidney, W.J.P. Millar, "The Salaries of Teachers in English Canada, 1900–1940: A Reappraisal," *Historical Studies in Education,* Spring 2010: 25, table 1]). In 1920, the average annual income in the United States was just under $3,270 (Treasury Department, US Internal Revenue, *Statistics of Income from Returns of Net Income for 1920* [Washington: Government Printing Office, 1922]: 2).

14. From a diagram prepared by Constable William Gibson, entitled "Plan of Tree River Detachment, April 1, 1922" and marked "Exhibit No. 1." RG 13 C-1, vol 1526, "Alikomiak," vol 1, Part 1. LAC.

15. From a scale map of the region prepared by Constable William Gibson and marked "Exhibit No. 2." RG 13 C-1, vol 1526, "Alikomiak," vol 1, Part 1. LAC.

16. Coates and Morrison, "'To Make These Tribes Understand,'" 105, claimed there were only four white men in the area. There were actually seven: Doak and his constables: J.H. Bonshor, D.H. Woolams and A. Stevenson; plus three HBC traders: C.H. Clarke, Otto Binder, and the outpost manager, Peter Norberg.

17. Harring, "The Rich Men of the Country," 7.

18. Knud Rasmussen, *Intellectual Culture of the Copper Eskimo* (Copenhagen: Gyldendalske Boghandel, 1932), 63.

19. Cortlandt Starnes, Assistant RCMP Commissioner. "Notes Re: Murder of Corporal W.A. Doak and Otto Binder at Tree River, on 1st. of April, 1992." Letter No. FT 2918, August 28, 1922. A.92/19/38, fol. 166–171, Hudson's Bay Company Archives (hereafter HBCA).

20. Doak's induction physical recorded his specifics and noted the presence of his tattoos. RCMP Service Record for William A. Doak, 1905–1921. RG 18-G, vol 3466, file 4396. LAC.

21. Coates and Morrison, "'To Make These Tribes Understand,'" 105–106.

Chapter Three: A Christian Crime

1. The RCMP crime reports relating to the massacre are all entitled "Shooting Affray." RG 18 vol 3293, vol 2. LAC.

2. "One of the toughest …" and "very quick with …" — Crime Report Re: Murder of Eskimo Native Pugnana, March 4, 1922. RG 13, vol 271, no. 1520. LAC.

3. Lisa Beiler, "Alikomiak and Tatamigana: Justice and Injustice in the Canadian Arctic," MA Thesis, University of Waterloo, 2016: 21.

4. Statement of Tatamigana, April 24, 1923. RG 18, vol 3289, file HQ-681-G-1. LAC.

5. The extramarital relationships were described in Tatamigana's statement to Stuart Wood, April 24, 1923, RG 13 C-1, vol 1526, vol 1, Part 1. LAC. In her MA thesis, Lisa Beiler challenges the translation of that statement, arguing it is unclear what Tatamigana was describing to investigators ("Alikomiak and Tatamigana: Justice and Injustice in the Canadian Arctic," footnote on page 22).

6. Crime Report Re: Tatamigana, by S.T. Wood. RG 18, vol 3289, file HQ-681-G-1. LAC.

7. Beiler: 22–23.

8. Beiler writes that Pugnana and Tatamigana did "the majority of the killing, though they were supported by the rest of the community."

9. The names of the victims and their familial relationships are detailed in Beiler (xiii). In her thesis, Beiler attributes responsibility for some of the deaths to individuals other than Pugnana and Tatamigana.

10. W.A. Doak, "Crime Report Re: Eskimo Tatamigana," March 4, 1922. RG 18, vol 3289, file HQ-6810G01. LAC. Although the proclamation

appears harsh, Beiler contends the Inuit perceived girls as "another mouth to feed." Until girls reached marrying age, they were often killed if their parents died (Beiller: 37).

11. Tatamigana's statement to police, April 24, 1923. RG 13 C-1, vol 1526, vol 1, Part 1. LAC.

12. Ibid.

13. M. Aupilaarjuk, M. Tulimaaq, A. Joamie, E. Imaruittuq, and L. Nutaraaluk, *Perspectives on Traditional Law* (Iqaluit: Nunavut Arctic College, 1999), 55.

14. Tatamigana's statement to police, April 24, 1923.

15. Beiler challenges White interpretations of the relationships between the players in her MA thesis ("Alikomiak and Tatamigana: Justice and Injustice in the Canadian Arctic," 30), arguing the translator had confused Western terms with Inuit notions of kinship. Alikomiak's father was Pugnana's brother and Tatamigana's mother was Pugnana's sister.

16. Aupilaarjuk et al., *Perspectives on Traditional Law*, 166.

17. According to the initial statements Alikomiak and Tatamigana gave to police, an eight-year-old boy — most likely Pugnana's own son — accompanied them on the hunting trip. The boy played no significant role in the shooting.

18. Tatamigana's statement to police, April 24, 1923.

19. S.T. Wood, RCMP Inspector, during his trial testimony. Transcript, *King v Alikomiak* (murder of Pugnana), July 17, 1923. RG 13 C-1, vol 1526, "Alikomiak," vol 1, Part 1. LAC.

20. S.T. Wood, "Crime Report: Murder of Eskimos at Kent Peninsula," August 29, 1921. RG 18, vol 3289, file HG-681-G-1. LAC.

Chapter Four: Worlds Collide

1. RCMP report, "General Conditions Eastern Arctic Coast," December 15, 1921. RG 18 vol 3289 file HQ-681-G-1. LAC.

2. Harwood Steele, *Policing the Arctic: The Story of the Conquest of the Arctic by the Royal Canadian (formerly North West) Mounted Police* (Toronto: Ryerson Press, 1936), 231.

3. Doak's report is contained in RG 18, vol 3289, file HQ-681-G-1. LAC.

4. Cortlandt Starnes, "Notes Re: Murder of Corporal W.A. Doak and Otto Binder at Tree River, on 1st. of April, 1922." A.92/19/38, folio 166–171. HBCA.

5. Starnes, "Notes Re: Murder of Corporal W.A. Doak and Otto Binder at Tree River, on 1st. of April, 1922."

6. Corporal Doak's Report of Patrol to Kent Peninsula for December 3, 1921 to January 2, 1922, quoted in *Report of the Royal Canadian Mounted Police for the Year Ended September 30, 1920* (Ottawa: F.A. Acland, 1921), 43–44.

7. Starnes, "Notes Re: Murder of Corporal W. A. Doak and Otto Binder at Tree River, on 1st of April, 1922."

8. Statement of Alikomiak, April 17, 1923.

9. Quoted in Philip H. Godsell, *They Got Their Man: On Patrol with the Northwest Mounted Police* (Toronto: Ryerson Press, 1932), 184.

10. Starnes, "Notes Re: Murder of Corporal W.A. Doak and Otto Binder at Tree River, on 1st of April, 1922."

Chapter Five: The Threat of the Mundane

1. In his letter to RCMP Edmonton Command, July 2, 1922 (RG vol 3293, 1922-HQ-681-G-4. LAC), Inspector Wood wrote: "Binder was very punctual in his morning calls about 8 am and it can safely be presumed this particular morning was no exception."

2. Vilhjalmur Stefansson, *The Friendly Arctic: The Story of Five Years in Polar Regions* (New York: MacMillan, 1921), 645.

3. Stefansson, *The Friendly Arctic*, 645, 669.

4. Stuart E. Jenness, *Stefansson, Dr. Anderson and the Canadian Arctic Expedition, 1913–1918: A Story of Exploration, Science and Sovereignty* (Ottawa: Mercury Series History Paper 56, Canadian Museum of Civilization, 2011), 201.

5. Letter from A. Brabant, Fur Trade Commissioners, to C. Starnes, July 24, 1922. RG 18, vol 3293, 1922-HQ-681-G-4. LAC.

6. From Binder's Hudson's Bay Company biography, RG 3/40A/2. HBCA. Other biographical details drawn from HBCA RG 2/4/74; and from a brief account of his death in Philip H. Godsell, *Arctic Trader: An Account of Twenty Years with the Hudson's Bay Company* (Toronto: MacMillan, 1946), 208–211.

7. Letter from Cortlandt Starnes to Mr. Gallagher, Dept. Of Justice, November 29, 1923. RG 18, vol 3293, file 1922-HQ-681-G-1, vol 2. LAC.

8. "Personal" letter from C. Starnes to M.F. Gallagher, November 28, 1923. RG 18, vol 3293, 1922-HQ-681-G-1, vol 2. LAC.

9. In her master's thesis, Lisa Beiler claims the relationship was beneficial to the couple themselves — she brought him local traders; he gave her access to trade goods — but the relationship caused tension within her village because it created an imbalance in the male-to-female ratio ("Alikomiak and Tatamigana: Justice and Injustice in the Canadian Arctic," University of Waterloo, 2016: 24.)

10. Alikomiak's statement to police, April 17, 1923. RG 13 C-1, vol 1526, "Alikomiak," vol 1, Part 1. LAC.

11. Letter from H. Milton Martin to J. Ritchie, December 31, 1924. RG, vol 3293, 1922-HQ-681-G-4. LAC.

12. Alikomiak's statement to police, April 17, 1923.

13. Ibid.

14. Statement of Cst. D.H. Woolams, cited in Crime Report by S.T. Wood, August 13, 1922. RG, vol 3293, 1922-HQ-681-G-4. LAC.

15. Starnes, "Notes Re: Murder of Corporal W.A. Doak and Otto Binder, at Tree River on 1st of April, 1922."

16. Alikomiak's statement to police, April 17, 1923.

17. In his statement to police, C.H. Clarke noted clear drag marks leading from the blood stain on the ice to the police barracks (statement dated April 15, 1922, RG 18, vol 3293, 1922-HQ-681-G-4. LAC).

18. Statement of Ayalegak, appended to S.T. Wood's Crime Report, August 13, 1923. RG 18, vol 3293, 1922-HQ-681-G-4. LAC.

19. Crime Report by J.H. Bonshor, April 8, 1922. RG 18, vol 3293, 1922-HQ-681-G-4. LAC.

20. Statement by Ayalegak, appended to S.T. Wood's Crime Report, August 13, 1923. Although Ayalegak specified they had placed Binder on Bonshor's bed, Bonshor stated Binder's body was found on Stevenson's bed (Crime Report by J.H. Bonshor, April 8, 1922. RG 18, vol 3293, 1922-HQ-681-G-4. LAC).

Chapter Six: A Cursory Investigation

1. Statement of Toktogan, April 14, 1922 (appended to J.H. Bonshor's Crime Report). RG 18, vol 3293, 1922-HQ-681-G-4. LAC.

2. Crime Report by J.H. Bonshor, April 8, 1922. RG 18, vol 3293, 1922-HQ-681-G-4. LAC.

3. Statement of C.H. Clarke, who was present in Woolams's house at the time. April 15, 1922. RG 18, vol 3293, 1922-HQ-681-G-4. LAC. There are varying accounts as to whether Woolams stayed in a tent or a snow house during his time at the seal camp. Woolams himself uses both terms in his numerous reports.

4. Ibid.

5. Constable Stevenson's "Report of Patrol from Tree River to Aklavik," July 29, 1922. RG 18, vol 3298, file 1922-HQ-681-G-1, vol 1. LAC.

6. Lisa Beiler argues that Alikomiak's continued freedom during his trip west cast "doubt on the perception that the RCMP considered [him] a threat" ("Alikomiak and Tatamigana: Justice and Injustice in the Canadian Arctic," MA Thesis, University of Waterloo, 2016: 115).

7. As quoted in Miriam Green Ellis, "Eskimos, Stoic, Unconcerned, Accept Fate Unprotestingly," *Toronto Daily Star*, November 28, 1923.

8. Letter from C. Starnes to Allison Doak, July 27, 1922. R196-158-9-E, 1905-1921. RG 18-G, vol 3466, file 4396. LAC.

9. The original telegram, as well as Starnes's response, are retained in Doak's RCMP Service Records, R196-158-9-E, 1905-1921. RG 18-G, vol 3466, file 4396. LAC.

10. See, for example, "Two White Men Are Slain by an Eskimo," *Manitoba Free Press*, July 22, 1922; "Mounted Constable is Killed by Eskimo," Toronto *Globe*, July 24, 1922; "Eskimo Murders Two in Far North," *Montreal Gazette*, July 24, 1922.

11. See, for example, "The Murderer of Corporal W. Doak Hated the Whites," *St. John Daily Telegraph*, July 26, 1922.

Chapter Seven: One Time Too Many

1. William B. Henderson, "Indian Act," *The Canadian Encyclopedia*, 2006. www.canadianencyclopedia.ca, accessed October 30, 2016.

2. Details of the case taken from Richard G. Condon, *The Northern Copper Inuit: A History* (Toronto: University of Toronto Press, 1996), 115; as well as Keith Ross Leckie, *Coppermine* (Toronto: Viking Canada, 2010); McKay Jenkins, *Bloody Falls of the Coppermine: Madness, Murder and the Collision of Cultures in the Arctic, 1913* (New York: Random House, 2006); Dennis Drabelle, "A Remarkable Record," *Pennsylvania Gazette* 103, no. 5 (2005): 13–17.

3. Ken S. Coates and William R. Morrison, "'To Make These Tribes Understand': The Trial of Alikomiak and Tatamigana," in *Strange Things Done: Murder in Yukon History* (Montreal: McGill-Queen's University Press, 2004), 104.

4. Sidney L. Harring, "'The Rich Men of the Country'": Canadian Law in the Land of the Copper Inuit, 1914–1930." *Ottawa Law Review* 21, no. 1 (1989): 7.

5. Letter from C. Starnes to D.C. Scott, October 20, 1923. RG 18, vol 3293, 1922-HQ-681-G-1, vol 1. LAC.

6. Cortlandt Starnes, "Murder of Corp. Doak, WA and Otto Binder by Copper Eskimo Alikomiak," July 21, 1922. RG, vol 3293, file 1922-HQ-681-G-1, vol 1. LAC.

7. Quoted in William Morrison, *Showing the Flag: The Mounted Police and Canadian Sovereignty in the North, 1894–1925* (Vancouver: University of British Columbia Press, 1985), 138.

Chapter Eight: Lucien and Herschel

1. *Minutes of the CNWT, 1936.* M-811-15. LAC.

2. Graham Price, "The King v Alikomiak," in Dale Gibson and W. Wesley Pue (eds.), *Glimpses of Canadian Legal History* (Winnipeg: Legal Research Institute of the University of Manitoba, 1991), 224.

3. Ibid.

4. Sidney L. Harring, "The Rich Men of the Country: Canadian Law in the Land of the Copper Inuit, 1914–1930," *Ottawa Law Review* 21, no. 1 (1989): 2–3.

5. Ken S. Coates and William R. Morrison, "'To Make These Tribes Understand,'" *Strange Things Done: Murder in Yukon History* (Montreal: McGill-Queen's University Press, 2004), 109.

6. Stuart Wood, "Location of Trials," RG 18, vol 3289, file HQ-681-G-1. LAC.

7. Cited in letter from Corstandt Starnes to E.L. Newcombe, April 25, 1923. RG 13, vol 271, 1519–1539, 1922. LAC.

8. Price, "The King v Alikomiak," 229.

9. See, for example, letter to Sir Lomer Gouin from S.W. Jacob, October 23, 1922, or letter from E.B. Cogswell to E.L. Newcombe, January 9, 1923, both contained in RG 13, vol 271, 1519–1539, 1922. LAC.

10. Letter from E.L. Newcombe to E.B. Cogswell, January 25, 1923. RG 13, vol 271, 1519–1539, 1922. LAC.

11. LeBeau was executed on November 1, 1921. Price, "The King v Alikomiak," 205.

12. Price, "The King v Alikomiak," 214.

13. Letter from E.L. Newcombe to C. Starnes, April 17, 1923. RG 13, vol 271, 1519–1539, 1922. LAC.

14. Price, "The King v Alikomiak," 214.

15. Ibid.

16. Letter from E.L. Newcombe to Lucien Dubuc, May 11, 1923. RG 18, vol 3293, 1922-HQ-681-G-1, vol 1. LAC.

17. As noted in a letter from E.L. Newcombe to C. Starnes, dated May 16, 1923. RG 13, vol 271, 1519–1539, 1922. LAC.

18. The law was not Howatt's sole source of income. He was also a director in a gold mining company and held an interest in another mining operation in British Columbia.

19. All biographical materials drawn from the entry for Irving Brass Howatt, in *Alberta, Past and Present, Historical and Biographical*, vol 3. Accessed May 20, 2017, www.electricscotland.com/history/canada/alberta/irving_howatt.htm.

20. Unlike the American system, in which the accused has the right to an attorney even if they cannot afford one, Canadians are not granted free legal representation. A lone exception is made for capital offences, in that the accused will be assisted in securing the services of a pro bono lawyer for the duration of the trial.

21. William R. Morrison, "Alikomiak" in *Dictionary of Canadian Biography*, vol 15. University of Toronto/Université Laval, 2003. www.biographi.ca/en/bio/Alikomiak_15E.html.

22. A photo of W.W. Cory can be found in a roster of "Former Deputy Ministers" maintained by Natural Resources Canada, www.nrcan.gc.ca/former-deputy-ministers/10861.

23. Letter from W.W. Cory to E.L. Newcombe, April 4, 1923. RG 13, vol 271, 1519–1539, 1922. LAC. Cory recommended barrister W.G. Harrison.

24. Memorandum from T. L. Cory to O.S. Finnie, dated September 12, 1922. RG 85, vol 607, file 2580. LAC.

25. Letter to T.L. Cory from E.L. Newcombe, May 16, 1923. RG 13, vol 271, 1519–1539, 1922. LAC.
26. Letter from E.L. Newcombe to I.B. Howatt, May 16, 1923. RG 13, vol 271, 1519–1539, 1922. LAC.
27. Letter from W.R. Lindsay to C. Starnes, May 22, 1923. RG 18, vol 3293, 1922-HQ-681-G-1, vol 1. LAC.

Chapter Nine: Impediments

1. RCMP memorandum, December 2, 1922. RG 13, vol 271, 1519–1539, 1922. LAC. The memo cites Section 586, ss 2 and ss 3 of the Criminal Code, which states NWT crimes cannot be tried in the Yukon Territory.
2. Letter from E.L Newcombe to Irving B. Howatt, May 16, 1923, RG18, vol 3293, file 1922-HQ-681-G-1 vol 1. LAC.
3. Bill 7 was first drafted with two amendments. The first amendment waived the requirement that the ten-man jury consist solely of British Subjects, clearing the way for Indigenous jurors. This amendment passed the House of Commons but was vetoed by the Senate. The second amendment empowered a circuit court magistrate to preside over an NWT case outside of the territorial boundary. It also granted leave to enforce the judgments and punishments — including executions — outside of the NWT. The second amendment was approved by both the House and the Senate. (Senate Debates [Hansard], NWT Bill 7 First Reading, March 1, 1923,14 Parliament, 2 Session, vol 1: 81; Senate Debates [Hansard], NWT Bill 7 Second Reading, March 8, 1923, 14 Parliament, 2 Session, vol 1: 104–105; Senate Debates [Hansard], NWT Bill 7 Considered in Committee Progress Report, March 13, 1923, 14 Parliament, 2 Session, vol 1: 151–157; Senate Debates [Hansard], "NWT Bill 7 Further Considered in Committee, March 15, 1923, 14 Parliament, 2 Session: 198–199.)
4. Jeffery Williams, *Byng of Vimy: General and Governor General* (London: Leo Cooper/Secker & Warburg, 1983), 5.
5. Governor General of Canada Archive, "Field Marshal, The Viscount Byng of Vimy," archive.gg.ca, accessed October 26, 2017.
6. Telegram from E.L. Newcombe to I.B. Howatt, June 8, 1923. RG 13, vol 271, 1519–1539, 1922. LAC.
7. Wood held his preliminary hearings on April 24, 1923. As of June 8 of

that same year, Byng had yet to sign Bill 7. The law could not be applied retroactively to make the preliminary hearings valid.

8. "Criminal Procedure," www.thecanadianencyclopedia.ca/en/article/ criminal-procedure/.

9. Letter from G.L. Jennings to C. Starnes, November 14, 1922. RG 18, vol 3293, 1922-HQ-681-G-1, vol 1. LAC.

10. Letter from E.L. Newcombe to T.L. Cory, May 16, 1923. RG 13, vol 271, 1519–1539, 1922. LAC. Mail delays hold some of the blame for the miscommunication. Wood held the preliminary hearings in April but "did not return in time to have these papers sent out by last winter mail." Instead he held the transcripts at Herschel until the judicial party arrived. (Letter from C. Starnes to E.L. Newcombe, April 25, 1923. RG 18, vol 3293, 1922-HQ-681-G-1, vol 1. LAC.)

11. Stuart Wood's Invoice for Services, September 9, 1924. RG 18, vol 3293, 1922-HQ-681-G-1, vol 2. LAC.

12. Letter from Cortlandt Starnes to E.L. Newcombe, November 4, 1924. RG 18, vol 3293, 1922-HQ-681-G-1, vol 2. LAC

13. Graham Price, "The King v Alikomiak" in Dale Gibson and W. Wesley Pue (eds.), *Glimpses of Canadian Legal History* (Winnipeg: Legal Research Institute of the University of Manitoba, 1991), 227.

Chapter Ten: Premeditation

1. Sir W. Mars-Jones, "Beeching — Before and After on the Wales and Chester Circuit," *Cambrian Law Review* 81, no. 1 (1972–1973): 82.

2. Letter from G.S. Worsley to RCMP Edmonton Command, May 31, 1923. RG 18, vol 3293, 1922-HQ-681-G-1, vol 1. LAC.

3. F.E. Spriggs, "Trip of Judicial Party from Edmonton to Herschel Island and Return," September 21, 1923. RG 18, vol 3293, file 1922-HQ-681-G1, vol 1. LAC.

4. Letter from C. Starnes to RCMP Commander Edmonton, May 31, 1923. RG 18, vol 3293, file 1922-HQ-681-G-1. LAC.

5. Report by Officer Spriggs, September 21, 1923. RG 18, vol 3293, 1922-HQ-681-G-1, vol 1. LAC.

6. See, for example, "Secret" letter from C. Starnes to RCMP Commander Montreal, May 31, 1923. RG 18, vol 3293, 1922-HQ-681-G-1, vol 1. LAC. In the letter, the commissioner wrote: "In his own interests, and

in the interests of discretion, the express intention of his engagement will not be disclosed to the Party, but if a hangman is required, he will volunteer for the duty at the proper time.... See that the purpose of his engagement are kept secret. You may consider it necessary to secretly inform Sgt. Spriggs ... but to no one else. He can inform Insp. Wood in the same way on his arrival to Herschel."

7. Letter from J. Ritchie to C. Starnes, September 15, 1923. RG 18, vol 3293, 1922-HQ-681-G-1, vol 1. LAC.
8. Letter from C. Starnes to the Officer Commanding RCMP Edmonton, May 31, 1923. RG 18 vol 3293, file 1922 HQ-681-6-11. LAC. Starnes recommended an addendum to the contract, stating "if a hangman is required, he will volunteer for the duty at the proper time."
9. "Secret" letter from Sgt. W.D.M. Henderson to RCMP Commander Montreal, May 17, 1923. RG 18, vol 3293, 1922-HQ-681-G-1, vol 1. LAC.
10. Confidential letter from A.J. Cawdron to RCMP Commander Lethbridge, April 24, 1923. See also letter from Christen Junget to Cortlandt Starnes, May 7, 1923. Unlike Gill, Wakelen "thoroughly understands he is to play the part of a special constable" and keep his mission secret ("Secret and personal letter" from C. Junget to C. Starnes, March 29, 1923). All sources in RG 18, vol 3293, 1922-HQ-681-G-1, vol 1. LAC.
11. "1921 The Trial of Albert LeBeau," Prince of Wales Northern Heritage Centre. www.nwttimeline.ca/1900/1921_LeBeau.htm.
12. Letter from Albert J. Cawdron to RCMP Commander Montreal, May 15, 1923. RG 18, vol 3293, 1922-HQ-681-G-1, vol 1. LAC.
13. "Secret and personal" letter from Junget to Starnes, March 29, 1923.
14. "Secret" letter from Cortlandt Starnes to Lethbridge Commander, March 23, 1923 (RG 18, vol 3293, 1922-HQ-681-G-1, vol 1. LAC).
15. Confidential letter from Christen Junget to C. Starnes, May 9, 1923. RG 18, vol 3293, 1922-HQ-681-G-1, vol 1. LAC.
16. "1921 The Trial of Albert LeBeau," Prince of Wales Northern Heritage Centre. www.nwttimeline.ca/1900/1921_LeBeau.htm.
17. Letter from J.W. Philips to C. Starnes, March 22, 1923. RG 18, vol 3293, 1922-HQ-681-G-1, vol 1. LAC.
18. "Secret" letter from J.W. Philips to RCMP Commander Montreal, May 17, 1923 and letter from J.W. Philips to C. Starnes, March 22, 1923.

Both in RG 18, vol 3293, 1922-HQ-681-G-1, vol 1. LAC. Although highly unconventional, the RCMP concurred with Ellis's desire to execute immediately following sentence. Commander Jennings wrote: "I was in hope that whatever judge was appointed" could be authorized by the government to move straight to hanging "within a reasonable time." Unfortunately, "as the law stands at present," execution upon verdict was not possible (Letter from G.L. Jennings to C. Starnes, April 19, 1923. RG 18, vol 3293, 1922-HQ-681-G-1, vol 1. LAC).

19. "Secret" letter from Sgt. W.D.M. Henderson to RCMP Commander Montreal, May 17, 1923. RG 18, vol 3293, 1922-HQ-681-G-1, vol 1. LAC.

20. Letter from C. Starnes to RCMP Commander Montreal, June 1, 1923. RG 18, vol 3293, 1922-HQ-681-G-1, vol 1. LAC. See also letter from G.S. Worsley to RCMP Commander, Montreal, June 1, 1923. RG 18, vol 3293, 1922-HQ-681-G-1, vol 1. LAC.

21. Letter from J.W. Philips, RCMP Quebec District to Commissioner Starnes, May 30, 1923. RG 18, vol 3293, file 1922-HQ-681-G-1, vol 1. LAC.

22. Confidential letter from Cortlandt Starnes to RCMP Commander Montreal, April 13, 1923. RG 18, vol 3293, 1922-HQ-681-G-1, vol 1. LAC.

23. Letter from Albert J. Cawdron, quoting Commissioner Starnes, to RCMP Commander, Montreal, May 15, 1923. RG 18, vol 3293, 1922-HQ-681-G-1, vol 1. LAC.

24. Ibid.

25. Letter from Cortlandt Starnes to Mr. Gallagher, 1923. RG 18, vol 3293, file 1922-HG-681-6-1, vol 3. LAC. Despite the extra income, Gill requested a cash advance from the RCMP shortly after arriving on Herschel because he had no idea how long he needed to stay in order to carry out the executions. The request was granted because, at that point, "his sojourn at Herschel is indefinite." Letter from J. Ritchie to Cortlandt Starnes, September 15, 1923. RG 18, vol 3293, 1922-HQ-681-G-1, vol 1. LAC.

26. Letter from G.L. Jennings to C. Starnes, April 19, 1923. RG 18, vol 3293, 1922-HQ-681-G-1, vol 1. LAC.

27. Carolyn Strange, "Capital Punishment," in Gerald Hallowell (ed.), *The Oxford Companion of Canadian History*, vol 1 (Toronto: Oxford University Press Canada, 2004), 115.

28. Confidential letter from Inspector Wood to Superintendent J. Ritchie of the Edmonton Detachment, February 10, 1924. RG 18, vol 3293, 1922-HQ-681-6-1, vol 2. LAC.

29. Letter from S.T. Wood to RCMP Edmonton Command, July 2, 1922. RG vol 3293, 1922-HQ-681-G-4. LAC.

30. Letter from I.B. Howatt to E.L. Newcombe, May 29, 1923. RG 13, vol 271, 1519–1539, 1922. LAC.

31. See, for example, letter from E.L. Newcombe to I.B. Howatt, June 5, 1923. RG 13, vol 271, 1519–1539, 1922. LAC.

32. Telegram from the Deputy Minister of Justice to Judge Lucien Dubuc, June 8, 1923. RG 85, vol 607, file 2580. LAC. The deputy minister also advised Dubuc to allow enough time between the presumed guilty verdict and the execution for the transcripts and evidence to make their way to Ottawa for final review.

33. Letter from S.T. Wood to Lucien Dubuc, August 10, 1923. RG 13, vol 1526, vol 1. LAC.

34. Louis-Jacques Dorais, *The Language of the Inuit: Syntax, Semantics and Society in the Arctic* (Montreal: McGill-Queen's University Press, 2010), 8–27. The complexities of the Inuit language and its major families and dialects cannot be understated. Numerous dialects were spoken in each region, as well as a form of Herschel Island "pidgin" that combined elements of each (Dorais, personal communication, 2017).

Chapter Eleven: Beyond Comprehension

1. Cortlandt Starnes replaced his predecessor Aylesworth Percy on April 1, 1923 — exactly one year after Corporal Doak's murder — becoming the seventh man to head the force. Starnes would hold the post until his retirement on July 31, 1931 (entry for Cortlandt Starnes, "Royal Canadian Mounted Police," www.britishempire.co.uk/forces/armyunites/canadiancavalry/rcmpstarnes.htm).

2. Letter from W.R. Lindsay to C. Starnes, May 22, 1923. RG 18, vol 3293, 1922-HQ-681-G-1, vol 1. LAC.

3. Letter from C. Starnes to RCMP Commander Edmonton, May 31, 1923. RG 18, vol 3293, 1922-HQ-681-G-1, vol 1. LAC. Starnes lacked the personal authority to order Dubuc to do anything, but was likely passing on information received from the Department of Justice.

4. Letter from RCMP Assistant Commissioner G.S. Worsley to Deputy Minister of Justice E.L. Newcombe, August 9, 1923. RG 13, vol 271, 1519–1539, 1922. LAC.

5. Report by Constable Woolams to RCMP Arctic Sub-District, May 8, 1923. RG 18 vol 3293, file 1922-HQ-681-G-1, vol 1. LAC.

6. Report by Sgt. Spriggs, September 21, 1923. RG 18, vol 3293, 1922-HQ-681-G-1, vol 1. LAC.

7. Graham Price, "The King v Alikomiak," in Dale Gibson and W. Wesley Pue (eds.) *Glimpses of Canadian Legal History* (Winnipeg: Legal Research Institute of the University of Manitoba, 1991), 218.

8. Letter from Cortlandt Starnes to Allison Doak, July 24, 1922. William Doak's Service Records, R196-158-9-E, 1905–1921. RG 18-G, vol 3466, file 4396. LAC.

9. Doak was shot on April 1, but no one south of the Arctic Circle knew of his death until almost four months later. The first inkling of trouble came in a telegram Starnes received from Major G.L. Jennings of the Edmonton detachment on July 21, 1922 (the original telegram, as well as Starnes's response, are retained in Doak's RCMP Service Records, R196-158-9-E, 1905–1921. RG 18-G, vol 3466, file 4396. LAC). Jennings had already heard rumours being spread by the crew of an HBC supply vessel. When a soon-to-be-discharged constable from Herschel Island arrived in Edmonton bearing official confirmation, Jennings immediately contacted headquarters.

10. Night letter from C. Starnes to RCMP Commander Winnipeg, July 25, 1922. R196-158-9-E, 1905–1921. RG 18-G, vol 3466, file 4396. LAC.

11. Letter from Allison Doak to C. Starnes, July 25, 1922. R196-158-9-E, 1905-1921. RG 18-G, vol 3466, file 4396. LAC.

12. For example, on April 27, 1922 — 26 days after Doak's death — explorer Vilhjalmur Stefansson wrote to the RCMP asking for Doak's Christian name and mailing address so he could send Doak a copy of his recent book. On May 1, 1922, Cortlandt Starnes wrote back providing Doak's contact information and thanking him in advance on Doak's behalf (Service Record for William A. Doak, R196-158-9-E, 1905-1921. RG 18-G, vol 3466, file 4396. LAC).

13. Memorandum from G. L. Jennings to C. Starnes, August 9, 1922. William Doak's Service Records, R196-158-9-E, 1905-1921. RG 18-G, vol 3466, file 4396. LAC.

14. See, for example, memorandum from C. Starnes to G.L. Jennings, August 16, 1922. William Doak's Service Records, R196-158-9-E, 1905-1921. RG 18-G, vol 3466, file 4396. LAC.

15. Letter from Percy W. Doak to James Ritchie, October 25, 1923. R196-158-9-E, 1905–1921. RG 18-G, vol 3466, file 4396. LAC.

16. Report by J.H. Bonshor, October 15, 1923. William Doak's Service Records, R196-158-9-E, 1905–1921. RG 18-G, vol 3466, file 4396. LAC.

17. Letter from Cortlandt Starnes to G.L. Jennings, July, 1922. William Doak's Service Records, R196-158-9-E, 1905-1921. RG 18-G, vol 3466, file 4396. LAC.

18. Crime Report Re: Murders of Reg. No. 4396 Corporal Doak, WA and Otto Binder by Eskimo prisoner Alikomiak, July 31, 1922. RG 18 vol 3293, file 1922-HQ-681-G-4. LAC.

19. Letter from G.L. Jennings to C. Starnes, July 31, 1922. RG vol, 3293, 1922-HQ-681-G-4. LAC.

20. Ibid.

21. Crime Report Re: Murders, July 31, 1922.

22. Letter from C.H. Clarke to the District Manager of the Hudson's Bay Company, Kittegazuit, April 15, 1922. A.92/19/38 fol 166–171. HBCA.

23. "Of no more value than $1.00" from a Letter from T.R. Caulkin to RCMP Edmonton Command, September 7, 1925. RG vol 3293, 1922-HQ-681-G-4. LAC. "Traded off most of his personal belongings while at Tree River" was taken from a Letter from Stuart Wood to RCMP Commander Edmonton, January 9, 1924. RG 18, vol 3293, 1922-HQ-681-G-1, vol 2. LAC. "Left whatever stuff was handed over to her" appears in a Letter from F.A. Barnes to S.T. Wood, July 31, 1925. RG vol 3293, 1922-HQ-681-G-4. LAC. Among the items were the "two cabinet photographs" of Otto Binder — the only known portraits of Binder — which have since disappeared from the public record.

24. Letter from Stuart Wood to RCMP Commander Edmonton, January 9, 1924. RG 18, vol 3293, 1922-HQ-681-G-1, vol 2. LAC.

25. Lisa Beiler, "Alikomiak and Tatamigana: Justice and Injustice in the Canadian Arctic," MA Thesis, University of Waterloo, 2016: 2–3. Ethnographer Rasmussen later documented examples of such infighting (Knud Rasmussen, *Intellectual Culture of the Copper Eskimo: Report of the*

Fifth Thule Expedition, 1921–1924, vol 9 [Copenhagen: Gyldendalske Boghandel, 1932], 18). Beiler contends that "Western outsiders" saw this endless squabbling over mates and the violence it spurred as a "problem of the Inuinnait culture," a problem they believed could be solved with another act of violence: the death penalty (42).

26. Corporal Doak, "Crime Report Re: Eskimo Tatamigana," March 4, 1922. RG 18, vol 3289, file HQ-681-G-1. LAC.

27. Letter from A. Brabant, HBC to A.B. Perry, RCMP, February 2, 1922. RG 18, vol 3289, file HQ-681-G-1. LAC.

Chapter Twelve: A More Likely Story

1. Stuart Wood, Crime Report Re: Tatamigana, August 13, 1923. RG 18, vol 3289. LAC.

2. Crime Report Re: Murders of Reg. No. 4396 Corporal Doak, WA and Otto Binder by Eskimo prisoner Alikomiak, July 31, 1922. RG 18 vol 3293, file 1922-HQ-681-G-4. LAC. Wood's reports were also far from perfect. In one of his earliest, Wood noted Doak was shot "through the abdomen" (S.T. Wood, "Notes re: murder of Cpl. W.A. Doak and Otto Binder by Eskimo Prisoner Alikomiak." Undated. RG 18, vol 3293, 1922-HQ-681-G-4. LAC).

3. Ibid.

4. Letter from S.T. Wood to RCMP Edmonton Command, July 2, 1922. RG, vol 3293, 1922-HQ-681-G-4. LAC. Wood also generated a diagram of the crime scene, appended to his report, that contradicted information included in the diagrams and report issued by Bonshor (Crime Report by S.T. Wood, August 13, 1923. RG, vol 3293, 1922-HQ-681-G-4. LAC).

5. Aupilaarjuk et al., *Perspective on Traditional Law,* 161.

6. William R. Morrison, *Showing the Flag: The Mounted Police and Canadian Sovereignty in the North, 1894–1925* (Vancouver: University of British Columbia Press, 1985), 136.

7. Statement of Alikomiak, April 17, 1923. RG 13, C-1, vol 1526, vol 1, Part 1. LAC.

8. Letter from S.T. Wood to RCMP Edmonton Command, July 2, 1922. RG, vol 3293, 1922-HQ-681-G-4. LAC.

9. The changes include the following: i) In a prior statement, Alikomiak

said he went back to the barracks "to get my cartridges which I knew were there" (Statement of Alikomiak, June 30, 1922. RG 18, vol 3293, 1922-HQ-681-G-4. LAC). In the new account, Alikomiak claimed the shells were with the gun in the storehouse; ii) In prior statements (April 10, 1922 and June 30, 1922. RG 18, vol 3293, 1922-HQ-681-G-4. LAC), Alikomiak claimed he did not know how old he was. Fearing the accused's age would be an issue, Wood interviewed Pete Norberg and obtained the HBC manager's estimate. During Alikomiak's third and final interrogation with Wood, Alikomiak claimed "I have seen Pete Norberg HBC trader at Kent Peninsula for four years"; iii) Bonshor and Woolams's initial reports both noted Alikomiak used his own gun to shoot Doak. Bonshor claimed Alikomiak shot Doak "in the back, with his own .30-30 rifle which had been placed in the storehouse after his arrest" (Crime Report by J.H. Bonshor, April 8, 1922. RG vol 3293, 1922-HQ-681-G-4. LAC). Wood replaced those statements with a new version in which Alikomiak killed Doak with an entirely different gun; iv) Alikomiak's understanding of spoken English changed dramatically. In his prior statement to police (June 30, 1922), Alikomiak did not understand what Doak said to him after he was shot. Once seated in front of Inspector Wood, Alikomiak now "understood [Doak] to say 'what is the matter with you?'"

10. Statement of Alikomiak, June 30, 1922.

11. Wood's invoice for his work as justice of the peace at the preliminary hearing charged $.150 (two hours) for his interrogation of Alikomiak. "Schedule of Fees for Sgt. Wood's Special Powers at the Herschel Trial." RG 18, vol 3293, vol 2. LAC.

12. Statement of Alikomiak, April 10, 1922.

13. Letter from S.T. Wood to RCMP Edmonton Command, July 2, 1922. RG, vol 3293, 1922-HQ-681-G-4. LAC.

14. Letter from C. Starnes to W.W. Cory, October 24, 1923, RG 85, vol 607 2580, 1923–1926. LAC.

Chapter Thirteen: An Unfortunate Choice of Hobby

1. The Lucien Dubuc fond at the Provincial Archive of Alberta is a treasure-trove of Dubuc's photos, ranging from family portraits and holiday snaps to ethnographic documentation of the Arctic culture and people.

2. Graham Price, "The King v Alikomiak," in Dale Gibson and W. Wesley Pue (eds.) *Glimpses of Canadian Legal History* (Winnipeg: Legal Research Institute of the University of Manitoba, 1991), 228–229.

3. Ibid, 230.

4. Judge Dubuc closing statements. Trial transcript, *King v Alikomiak* (murders of Binder and Doak), July 18, 1923. RG 13 C-1, vol 1526 "Alikomiak," vol 1, Part 1. LAC.

5. A letter from Lucien Dubuc to the Department of the Secretary of State, September 29, 1923. RG 13 C-1, vol 1526, "Alikomiak," vol 1, Part 1, CC 207, No. 24861. LAC.

6. John A. Yogis, *Barron's Canadian Law Dictionary*, 5th ed. (New York: Barron's Educational Series, 2003), 94–95. The definition of embracery includes contriving to have a jury comprising persons who are predisposed toward a specific verdict. Embracery was a common-law misdemeanour (established in *R v Leblanc*, 1885) when Dubuc held court, and has since been enshrined in the Criminal Code (s. 139(3), 1985, c. C-46). Graham Price ("The King v Alikomiak" in Dale Gibson and W. Wesley Pue (ed.), *Glimpses of Canadian Legal History* [Winnipeg: Legal Research Institute of the University of Manitoba, 1991], 228–229) was arguably the first legal scholar to accuse Dubuc of jury packing. Also, in 1921, the law required only that jurors be "British citizens," raising a significant legal issue: If the Inuit were not citizens under Canadian law, what gave the government the power to impose its laws upon the Inuit?

7. Report by Sgt. Spriggs, September 21, 1923. RG 18, vol 3293, 1922-HQ-681-G-1, vol 1. LAC. Poirier has been erroneously identified as Dubuc's law clerk (Sidney L. Harring, "The Rich Men of the Country: Canadian Law in the Land of the Copper Inuit, 1914–1930," *Ottawa Law Review* 21, no. 1 [1989], 15, footnote 46) and "a law student from Edmonton" (Price, "The King v Alikomiak," 221). At the time he joined the judicial party in Fort Norman, Poirier was a resident of the Northwest Territories. There is nothing to indicate he was ever a law student in Edmonton or anywhere else, and no records of him clerking for Dubuc. No record indicates Dubuc and Poirier knew each other before meeting in Fort Norman.

8. Letter from E.L. Newcombe to C. Starnes, April 17, 1923. RG 13, vol 271, 1519–1539, 1922. LAC.

9. Price, "The King v Alikomiak," 221.

10. Poirier's account appeared in the *Edmonton Journal* on September 29, 1923, although Harring claims to have seen a similar (or identical) report in the *Montreal Star* on September 15, 1924. (Harring, "The Rich Men of the Country," 15).

11. Yet another subheading to Poirier's account read "Herschel Island Post a Turmoil of Excitement during Murder Trials," *Edmonton Journal*, September 29, 1923.

12. The Jury Act of the NWT (RSNWT 1988c, J-2) holds that every juror must "well and truly keep secret the Queen's counsel … and every juror who divulges such secret is guilty of an offence" (SNWT 2015, c5, s8[1]).

13. Invoice for juryman services of Paul Poirier. RG 13, vol 271, 1519–1539, 1922. LAC. The trials ran from July 16 through 20 followed by the penalty phase on August 11 for a total of six courtroom days (Report by Sgt. Spriggs, September 21, 1923. RG 18, vol 3293, 1922-HQ-681-G-1, vol 1. LAC.) Poirier invoiced for a total of 61 days from July to September 1923.

14. That Dubuc was responsible for staging the photo is undeniable. Virtually identical images of his judicial parties in front of their makeshift courthouses were created for his 1921 trial of LeBeau and his subsequent Arctic trial in 1924 (see, for example, image A3663, Lucien Dubuc Fonds, Provincial Archives of Alberta).

Chapter Fourteen: All Evidence to the Contrary

1. Harwood Steele, *Policing the Arctic: The Story of the Conquest of the Arctic by the Royal Canadian (Formerly North-West) Mounted Police* (Toronto: Ryerson Press, 1936), 237.

2. Sidney L. Harring, "The Rich Men of the Country: Canadian Law in the Land of the Copper Inuit, 1914–1930," *Ottawa Law Review* 21, no. 1 (1989), 20, citing an article published in the *Montreal Star* on September 15, 1924.

3. Indictments of Tatamigana and Alikomiak — that they "at a certain place … on or about September 1921 did murder Pugnana" — and Indictment for Alikomiak — for killing Doak and Binder on April 1, 1922 in Tree River — all issued July 16, 1923, signed by I.B. Howatt. RG 13, vol 1526, vol 1. LAC.

4. Howatt's last-minute indictments were likely generated to solve another problem: the lack of any credible mechanism charging the accused with their crimes. An unsigned partial carbon copy of a memo retained in the RCMP file suggested it was possible to substitute a formal charge by police in lieu of an indictment, although Criminal Code section 873 A notes that the Attorney General must approve such a manoeuvre. There is no indication the RCMP pursued this option, and no record of the AG receiving or approving such a request (RCMP memorandum, December 2, 1922. RG 13, vol 271, 1519–1539, 1922. LAC). Howatt produced the indictments when he realized there was no mechanism in place that rendered the arrest and prosecution of Alikomiak and Tatamigana lawful.

5. Bryan A. Garner (ed.), *Black's Law Dictionary* (St. Paul: West Group, 2001), 314.

6. Under Canadian law, "the great writ" of *habeas corpus* applies to every defendant but only empowers a judge to order the release of a prisoner because of insufficient evidence or procedural failing. It "cannot be used to nullify" a verdict after the fact (John A. Yogis, *Barron's Canadian Law Dictionary,* 5th ed. [New York: Barron's Educational Series, 2003], 124). Dubuc should have recognized there were serious procedural issues with the preliminary hearings. He was empowered to stop the trials before they began to address the issue, but he did not.

7. Transcripts may have been produced but are not part of the Department of Justice files retained at the national archives. Case files, including transcripts, were only sent to Ottawa for review in death penalty cases.

8. Report by Sgt. Spriggs, September 21, 1923. RG 18, vol 3293, 1922-HQ-681-G-1, vol 1. LAC. Other accounts suggest Dubuc held off sentencing until August 11.

9. Lisa Beiler, "Alikomiak and Tatamigana: Justice and Injustice in the Canadian Arctic," MA Thesis, University of Waterloo, 2016: 14.

10. Aupilaarjuk et al., *Perspectives on Traditional Law*, 53.

11. Graham Price, "The King v Alikomiak," in Dale Gibson and W. Wesley Pue (eds.) *Glimpses of Canadian Legal History* (Winnipeg: Legal Research Institute of the University of Winnipeg, 1991), 29.

12. "Personal" letter from Howatt to E.L. Newcombe, September 25, 1926. RG 13, vol 271. LAC.

13. Trial transcript, *King v Alikomiak* (murder of Pugnana), July 17, 1923. RG 13 C-1, vol 1526, "Alikomiak," vol 1, Part 1. LAC.

14. Trial transcript, *King v Alikomiak* (murders of Binder and Doak). RG 13 C-1, vol 1526, "Alikomiak," vol 1, Part 1. LAC.

15. W. Rasing, *Too Many People: Order and Non-Conformity in Iglulingmiut Social Process* (Nijmegen: Katholieke Universiteit, Faculteit der Rechtsgeleerdheid, 1994), 134.

16. Beiler, 52. Traditional Inuit law held that "if the person was remorseful for his act and worked to be part of the community, you could let him live and be a part of the camp again," whereas "If you thought they were going to do it again, that person could be killed" (Aupilaarjuk et al., *Perspectives on Traditional Law,* 160).

17. Statement of Tatamigana re: Kent Peninsula. RG vol 3289, HQ-681-G-1. LAC.

18. Letter from Stuart Wood to G.L. Jennings, July 5, 1923. RG 18, vol 3293, 1922-HQ-681-G-1, vol 1. LAC. Starnes had appointed Wood sheriff on June 1, 1923, in a desperate bid to plug some of the jurisdictional holes in the case. The appointment empowered Wood to serve specific court functions during the upcoming trials, including overseeing prisoner detention and evidence handling.

19. Statement of Alikomiak, April 17, 1923. RG 13, C-1, vol 1526, vol 1, Part 1. LAC. Graham Price called Wood's dual roles at the time of the interrogation a clear conflict of interest ("The King v Alikomiak," 226).

20. Philip Bryden and Jula Hughes outlined the six categories of violations that call for disqualification of Canadian justices. Any judge who "has acquired knowledge of or been involved in the litigation in some capacity other than a judicial capacity" must be disqualified ("Legal Principles Governing Disqualification of Judges, www.papers.ssrn.com, 2014: 44). Wood's prior investigation and his interrogation of the prisoners, leading to their third and final confessions, had such knowledge and involvement, thereby disqualifying him to sit in a judicial capacity on the case.

21. Crime Report by S.T. Wood, August 13, 1923. RG, vol 3293, 1922-HQ-681-G-4. LAC.

22. "Criminal Procedure," www.thecanadianencyclopedia.ca/en/article/criminal-procedure/.

23. Cheryl Stephens, "You Have the Right to Remain Baffled: Plain Language and Criminal Justice," *Clarity* 69, no. 18 (2012): 18.

24. In Canada, the rights of arrestees and prisoners are protected under the Charter of Rights and Freedoms, enacted 1982 (www.charterofrights.ca/en/26_00_01, accessed May 4, 2017). When Wood interrogated Alikomiak and Tatamigana, the only laws in force came from Canada's original constitution, the British North America Act of 1867, which contained no "bill of rights" or express statements regarding the rights of detainees (www.charterofrights.ca/history).

25. Nowhere in any of Wood's notes, reports, the court documentation of the preliminaries, or even in private correspondence does he state that the prisoners entered a plea. It is a basic requirement that such a plea be clearly stated in the transcript or summary of the proceedings.

26. Wilfrid Laurier's Executive Order-in-Council, July 21, 1908. MG 266 C 865 vol 527–531. LAC.

27. James E. Hamby, James W. Thorpe, "The History of Firearm and Tool Mark Identification," *Association of Firearm and Tool Mark Examiners Journal* 31, no. 3 (1999): 7–12. Rifling had been routinely admissible in court since 1902.

28. Letter from S.T. Wood to RCMP Edmonton Command, July 2, 1922. RG 18 vol 3293, 1922-HQ-681-G-4. LAC.

29. Yogis, *Barron's Canadian Law Dictionary*, 31. The "best evidence" precedent was set in 1740.

30. A bewildered Wood wrote his superiors: "It is most disappointing that all these people were not sent out on the schooner as the [HBC] were quite willing to carry them" (Letter from Stuart Wood to RCMP Command, Edmonton, September 9, 1922. RG 18, vol 3293, 1922-HQ-681-G-1, vol 1. LAC).

31. S.T. Wood, "Notes re: murder of Cpl. W.A. Doak and Otto Binder by Eskimo Prisoner Alikomiak." Undated. RG 18, vol 3293, 1922-HQ-681-G-4. LAC.

32. Yogis, *Barron's Canadian Law Dictionary*, 66.

33. Garner, *Black's Law Dictionary*, 149.

34. John Sopinka, Sidney Lederhan, Alan Bryant, *The Law of Evidence in Canada*, 2nd ed. (Toronto: Butterworths, 1999), 234–247.

35. Howatt understood his prosecution in the Pugnana trials was deficient,

and he scrambled to correct the shortcomings in the far more crucial trial of Alikomiak for the murders of Doak and Binder. Witnesses, including Woolams, Wood, Toktogan, and Cyril, were called to testify as to the existence of the victims. Woolams described their injuries which, combined with the overstated certainty of Dr. Doyle's testimony, provided the causes of their deaths. While the evidence presented was not scientific, it arguably fulfilled the corpus delicti requirements for that specific trial.

36. Cortlandt Starnes was likely the author of the anonymous memo. The language and content of the memo suggests its content creator was a lawyer or judge, but Starnes probably took the comments and recommendations of that legal scholar and crafted them into a memo intended for internal RCMP use.

37. Letter from C. Starnes to W.W. Cory, October 24, 1923, RG 85, vol 607 2580, 1923–1926. LAC.

38. RCMP memorandum, "Re: Esquimaux at Herschell [*sic*] Island," December 2, 1922. RG 13, vol 271, 1519–1539, 1922. LAC.

39. U.S. rules regarding hearsay — Garner, *Black's Law Dictionary*, 106. The only Canadian hearsay exception rule arguably applicable was the "declaration against the defendant's interest" (Yogis, *Barron's Canadian Law Dictionary*, 125).

40. The memo made other questionable recommendations. In the killing of Hannak, the author feared the case against Tatamigana was weak and he would likely be acquitted. The memo recommended charging another Inuit named Ikalukpiak with the murder. Ikalukpiak "denies the crime" but, as the anonymous author noted, "there are no eye-witnesses" (RCMP memorandum, "Re: Esquimaux at Herschell [*sic*] Island," December 2, 1922. RG 13 vol 271, 1519–1539, 1922. LAC). The charges against Tatamigana remained, and he was later convicted and sentenced to five years incarceration.

Chapter Fifteen: Ineffective Counsel

1. Graham Price, "The King v Alikomiak," in Dale Gibson and W. Wesley Pue (eds.), *Glimpses of Canadian Legal History* (Winnipeg: Legal Research Institute of the University of Manitoba, 1991), 225.

2. No trial transcript survives of this portion of the proceedings, but the incident was reported in the trial coverage in the *Montreal Star* on

September 15, 1924, as well as in the *Edmonton Journal* on September
14, 1924. Sidney Harring cites the incident as an example of Dubuc's
significant technical errors during the trial, claiming Clarke's removal
resulted in a "mistrial" ("The Rich Men of the Country: Canadian Law
in the Land of the Copper Inuit, 1914–1930," *Ottawa Law Review* 21,
no. 1 (1989): 15).

3. Clarke's invoice, dated August 15, 1923. RG 13, vol 271, 1519–1539,
    1922. LAC. Dubuc's pencilled signature and typewritten notes appear
    on the bottom.

4. Trial transcript, *King v Alikomiak* (re murders of Doak and Binder), July
    18, 1923. RG 13, vol 1526, vol 1. LAC. Doak had two prior physicals
    — his induction physical in Calgary on June 2, 1905 and his "re-up"
    physical in Regina on July 4, 1911. Neither were conducted by Doyle.
    Doak had reengaged with the RCMP on July 4, 1921 for a three-year
    contract, but there is no record of a physical being conducted — by
    Dr. Doyle or any other person — at that time. The last medical note in
    his file is dated August 14, 1922. It is a discharge summary, signed by
    Cortlandt Starnes, that notes Doak was discharged as a consequence
    of "having died" on April 1, 1922. The absence of any note regarding
    Doyle's physical is a true anomaly. Doak's service records are exhaus-
    tively complete and extend through July 14, 1964 (R196-158-9-E,
    1905–1921. RG 18-G, vol 3466, file 4396. LAC).

5. Trial transcript, *King v Alikomiak*, July 18, 1923.

6. Ibid.

7. Ibid.

8. Ken S. Coates and William R. Morrison, "'To Make These Tribes
    Understand,'" *Strange Things Done: Murder in Yukon History* (Montreal:
    McGill-Queen's University Press, 2004), 111.

9. Coates and Morrison wrote that "one would not have to be a conspiracy
    theorist to suppose that the main reason he was appointed was that he
    was not expected to overexert his talents on behalf of the accused or
    make emotional post-trial statements in the press" ("'To Make These
    Tribes Understand,'" 111).

10. Judge Dubuc in a letter to E.L. Newcombe, September 22, 1923. RG
    13 C-1, vol 1526. LAC, in which Dubuc noted he had "nothing to
    complain of any action on the part of Mr. Cory."

11. Price, "The King v Alikomiak," 220.

12. Price, "The King v Alikomiak," 226. Price, a Calgary-based Queen's Counsel with more than forty years' experience litigating professional negligence, criticized Cory for failing to object to blatant hearsay. Sidney L. Harring also had harsh words for Cory's performance ("'The Rich Men of the Country,'" 12). Historians and anthropologists agree Cory's defence was non-existent (Coates and Morrison, "'To Make These Tribes Understand,'" 111; and Lisa Beiler, "Alikomiak and Tatamigana: Justice and Injustice in the Canadian Arctic," MA Thesis, University of Waterloo, 2016).

13. Suicide-by-cop occurs when a subject engages in aggressive or threatening behaviour with the intent of provoking police to use deadly force (K. Mohandie, J.R. Meloy, and P.I. Collins, "Suicide-by-Cop Among Officer-Involved Shooting Cases," *Journal of Forensic Sciences* 54, no. 2 (2009): 456).

14. Alikomiak's statement to police, April 17, 1923, RG 13 C-1, vol 1526, vol 1, Part 1. LAC, as well as Wood's testimony from the trial transcript, *King v Alikomiak* (for the murders of Doak and Binder), July 18, 1923. RG 13 C-1, vol 1526, "Alikomiak" vol 1, Part 1. LAC.

15. Letter from I.B. Howatt to E.L. Newcombe, September 25, 1923. RG 13, vol 271, 1519–1539, 1922. LAC.

16. The case has been the subject of serious scholarly review by Lisa Beiler, "Alikomiak and Tatamigana: Justice and Injustice in the Canadian Arctic," MA Thesis, University of Waterloo, 2016; Ken S. Coates, William R. Morrison, "'To Make These Tribes Understand': The Trial of Alikomiak and Tatamigana," in *Strange Things Done: Murder in Yukon History* (Montreal: McGill-Queen's University Press) 2004; Sidney L. Harring, "The Rich Men of the Country: Canadian Law in the Land of the Copper Inuit, 1914–1930," *Ottawa Law Review* 21, no. 1 (1989): 1–64; and Graham Price, "The King v Alikomiak," in Dale Gibson and W. Wesley Pue (eds.), *Glimpses of Canadian Legal History* (Winnipeg: Legal Research Institute of the University of Manitoba, 1991), 213–235. In addition, the case has featured prominently in popular accounts, including Daniel Campbell, "An Arctic Kangaroo Court: The Spectacle of Canada's First Trial in the Far North Was Little More Than a Show of Force," *Up Here Magazine* (April 2015): 92–93; Robert Collier

Fetherstonhaugh, *The Royal Canadian Mounted Police* (New York: Carrick and Evans, 1938); Philip H. Godsell, *Arctic Trader: The Account of Twenty Years with the Hudson's Bay Company* (Toronto: MacMillan, 1946); Kenn Harper, "Taissumani: A Day in Arctic History Feb. 1, 1924 The Only Hanging of Inuit In Canada," *Nunatsiaq News* (January 27, 2006); and Harwood Steele, *Policing the Arctic: The Story of the Conquest of the Arctic by the Royal Canadian (formerly North-West) Mounted Police* (Toronto: Ryerson Press, 1936). Without exception, all writers convey their belief that Alikomiak's confession was legitimate and that he murdered Doak and Binder. Graham Price believed Alikomiak's confession because it mirrored prior statements made by Sinnisuik and Uloqsaq (Price, "The King v Alikomiak," 232). Coates and Morrison reached a similar conclusion ("'To Make These Tribes Understand,'" 107–108).

17. Harwood Steele, *Policing the Arctic: The Story of the Conquest of the Arctic by the Royal Canadian (Formerly North-West) Mounted Police* (Toronto: Ryerson Press, 1936), 237.

18. Coates and Morrison, "'To Make These Tribes Understand,'" 107.

Chapter Sixteen: Intermediate Targets

1. C.A. Morgan, G.A. Hazlett, T. Doran, S. Garrett, G. Hoyt, P. Thomas, M. Baranoski, and S.M. Southwick, "Accuracy of Eyewitness Memory for Persons Encountered During Exposure to Highly Intense Stress," *International Journal of Law and Psychiatry* 27, no. 3 (2004): 265–279; B.L. Cutter and S.D. Penrod, *Mistaken Identification: The Eyewitness, Psychiatry and the Law* (New York: Cambridge University Press, 1995).

2. No specific weapon make or manufacturer was noted in any of the police reports. However, Alikomiak could only have obtained the gun through the HBC, and the only available guns matching that description were the L5037 or the L5058 — both 20-inch, round barrel, 7-shot carbines (S. James Gooding, *Trade Guns of the Hudson's Bay Company, 1670–1970* [Bloomfield ON: Historical Arms New Series No. 2, Museum Restoration Service, 2004]. See also *The Hudson's Bay Company Autumn and Winter Catalogue, No. 58, 1910–1911* [Winnipeg: Watson & Dwyer Publishing, reprinted 1977: 212–213]). The HBC discontinued its catalogue in 1912 (ibid: introduction, no page).

3. Although every crime report and confession by the accused stated "the

rifle had been fired through one of the upper panes of the barrack window facing the Company house," Harring ("'The Rich Men of the Country': Canadian Law in the Land of the Copper Inuit, 1914–1930," *Ottawa Law Review* 21, no. 1 [1989]: 12) claimed the window pane was first "broken out by the muzzle of the rifle" before the shot was fired. Harring freely admitted he based his accounts of the crime on newspaper reports and the "often exaggerated" reports of Philip H. Godsell (*They Got Their Man: On Patrol with the Northwest Mounted Police* [Toronto: Ryerson Press, 1932]) as "no transcripts remain" from the original trials (Harring, 13). The trial transcripts were readily available at the National Archives in Ottawa (now LAC) at the time Harring wrote his critique.

4. In his first statement to police, Alikomiak claimed Binder did not die right away. Binder screamed when he was hit and tried to get up but could not. By the time Alikomiak got to him on the ice, he was still breathing (Statement by Alikomiak, April 10, 1922. RG 18, vol 3293, 1922-HQ-681-G-4. LAC). In subsequent statements, Binder dies before Alikomiak reaches him.

5. S.N. Kunz, B.M. Zinka, S. Fieseller, M. Graw, and O. Peschel, "Laminated Safety Glass as an Intermediate Target: A Ballistic Study," *Journal of Forensic Sciences* 57, no. 5 (2012): 1246; see also W.W. Harper, "Behaviour of Bullets Fired Through Glass," *Journal of Criminal Law and Criminology* 29, no. 5, (1939): 718. The yaw, deformation of the bullet, and alteration of its flight path also impact the wounds produced. Bullets passing through glass create atypical or "keyhole" entrance wounds (Vincent JM Di Maio, *Gunshot Wounds: Practical Aspects of Firearms, Ballistics, and Forensic Techniques*, 2nd ed. [Boca Raton: CRC Press, 1999]: 100; Harper, "Behaviour of Bullets Fired Through Glass," 722–723). That Binder had no such wound is further evidence that Alikomiak's story is not accurate.

6. Harper, "Behaviour of Bullets Fired Through Glass," 720–723.

7. See, for example, J.I. Thornton, P.J. Cashman, "The Effect of Tempered Glass on Bullet Trajectory," *Journal of Forensic Sciences* 31, no. 2 (1986): 743–746; B.R. Burnett, "A Shot Through the Window," *Journal of Forensic Sciences* 46, no. 2 (2001): 379–385; C. Stahl, S.R. Jones, F.B. Johnson, and J.L. Luke, "The Effect of Glass as an Intermediate Target on Bullets: Experimental Studies and Report of a Case," *Journal of Forensic*

Sciences 24 (1979): 6–17; E.T. Miller, "Forensic Glass Comparison," in R. Saferstein (ed.), *Forensic Science Handbook* (Englewood Cliffs: Prentice-Hall, 1982), 139–183. Even at short-range distances, such as a bullet fired through a car window at its occupants, the bullet may strike the person but will miss its intended target.

8. J.D. Gunther and C.O. Gunther, *The identification of Firearms from Ammunition Fired Therein, with an Analysis of Legal Authorities* (New York: John Wiley and Sons, 1935), introduction. The Bureau of Ballistic Forensics opened in New York City the same year Alikomiak stood trial.

9. Statement of D.H. Woolams, cited in Crime Report by S.T. Wood, August 13, 1923. RG, vol 3293, 1922-HQ-681-G-4. LAC.

10. Statement by Mr. Clarke, April 15, 1922. RG 18, vol 3293, 1922-HQ-681-G-4. LAC.

11. W.U. Spitz and D.J. Spitz, *Spitz and Fisher's Medicolegal Investigation of Death: Guidelines for the Application of Pathology to Crime Investigation,* 4th ed. (Springfield: Charles C. Thomas Publishing, 2006), 105.

12. K.S. Wardak, S.J. Cina, "Algor Mortis: An Erroneous Measurement Following Postmortem Refrigeration," *Journal of Forensic Sciences* 56, no. 5 (2011): 1219–1221.

13. Report by Stuart Wood, July 1, 1922. RG 18, vol 3293, 1922-HQ-681-G-1, vol 1. LAC.

14. Search results for Tree River region, April 1, 1922; www.timeanddate.com.

15. Statement of Toktogan for the preliminary hearing, cited in Crime Report by S.T. Wood, August 13, 1923. RG, vol 3293, 1922-HQ-681-G-4. LAC.

16. Statement by C.H. Clarke, April 15, 1922. RG 18, vol 3293, 1922-HQ-681-G-4. LAC. In their initial statements, both Clarke and Woolams claimed two panes of the window contained bullet holes. After Wood assumed the role of lead investigator on the case, their statements were amended to only one broken window pane.

17. Pertinent studies have recently been conducted on algor mortis on human remains in subzero temperatures. See, for example, G. Mall, M. Hubig, M. Eckl, A. Buettner, and W. Eisenmenger, "Modelling Postmortem Surface Cooling in Continuously Changing Environmental Temperatures," *Legal Medicine* 4 (2002): 164–173; also G. Mall, M. Eckl,

I. Sinicina, O. Peschel, and M. Hubig, "Temperature-based Death Time Estimation with Only Partially Known Environmental Conditions," *International Journal of Legal Medicine* 119, no. 4 (2005): 185–194; and G. Mall, M. Hubig, G. Beler, A. Buettner, and W. Eisenmenger, "Determination of Time-Dependent Skin Temperature Decrease Rates in the Case of Abrupt Changes in Environmental Temperature," *Forensic Science International* 113, nos. 1–3 (2000): 219–226.

18. Wardak and Cina, "Algor Mortis: An Erroneous Measurement Following Postmortem Refrigeration," 1219–1221.

19. Statement of D.H. Woolams, cited in Crime Report by S.T. Wood, August 13, 1923.

20. Several formulas allow investigators to calculate time-since-death based on algor. Body temperature remains constant for the first forty-five to sixty minutes after death, a period known as the plateau. After the plateau, the body cools by 2 to 2.5 degrees per hour for the first twelve hours, then 1 degree/hour for the next six hours. The skin and limbs cool first. Although Woolams and Clarke's touch tests are the only available data, it is not the most accurate measure. Today, body temperature must be measured internally, requiring multiple readings of deep rectal or liver over a period of time following the discovery of a body (W.U. Spitz and D.J. Spitz, *Spitz and Fisher's Medicolegal Investigation of Death: Guidelines for the Application of Pathology to Crime Investigation*, 4th ed. [Springfield: Charles C. Thomas Publishing, 2006], 95). Other external factors can impact algor development. Ambient temperature plays the greatest role: the higher the gradient between body temperature and environment temperature, the faster the heat loss. Wind or "active air currents" also accelerate algor development (ibid, 96).

21. Spitz and Spitz, *Spitz and Fisher's Medicolegal Investigation of Death*, 101.

22. Ibid.,105.

23. Knud Rasmussen, *Intellectual Culture of the Copper Eskimo: Report of the Fifth Thule Expedition, 1921–1924*, vol 9 (Copenhagen: Gyldendalske Boghandel, 1932), 18. Wood was well aware of Rasmussen's studies, citing them in his own reports (Erhard Treude, "The Work of Knud Rasmussen in the Canadian Arctic as Described by RCMP Inspector Stuart Wood" in *Etudes/Inuit/Studies* 28, no. 2 [2004]: 186–201).

24. Wood's report reprinted verbatim in Treude, "The Work of Knud

Rasmussen in the Canadian Arctic as Described by RCMP Inspector Stuart Wood," 186–201.

25. Quoted in Harwood Steele, *Policing the Arctic: The Story of the Conquest of the Arctic by the Royal Canadian (Formerly North-West) Mounted Police* (Toronto: Ryerson Press, 1936), 227.

26. Confidential letter from A. Brabant to RCMP Commissioner, August 12, 1922. RG 18, vol 3293, 1922-HQ-681-G-4. LAC.

27. Letter from Lucien Dubuc to the Secretary of State, September 29, 1923. RG 13 C-1, vol 1526, vol 1. CC207, No. 24861. LAC.

28. As recounted in Rasmussen's journals, cited in Kenn Harper, "Taissumani: More on the Herschel Island Hangings," *Nunatsiaq News*, February 3, 2006.

29. Kenn Harper, "Taissumani, February 1, 1924: The Only Hanging of Inuit in Canada," *Nunatsiaq News*, January 27, 2006.

30. The incident was recounted in the Statement of Cyril Uingnek, cited in the Crime Report by S.T. Wood, August 13, 1923. RG vol 3293, 1922-HQ-681-G-4. LAC. Cyril was present at the seal camp when Alikomiak was first taken into custody and overheard the conversation.

31. Statement of Ayalegak, cited in the Crime Report by S.T. Wood, August 13, 1923. RG vol 3293, 1922-HQ-681-G-4. LAC.

32. A number of prior researchers have invoked *ilira* within the context of murder investigations. See, for example, Shelagh Grant, *Arctic Justice* (Montreal: McGill-Queen's University Press, 2002), 237–238; Hugh Brody, *The Other Side of Eden: Hunter-Gatherers, Farmers and the Shaping of the World* (London: Faber and Faber, 2001), 43. Lisa Beiler believes *ilira* might explain why the Inuit witnesses in this case continually changed their accounts ("Alikomiak and Tatamigana: Justice and Injustice in the Canadian Arctic," MA Thesis, University of Waterloo, 2016: 108).

Chapter Seventeen: Open to Interpretation

1. Letter from H. Milton Martin, executor of Doak's estate, to G.L. Jennings, October 23, 1923. According to Martin, Doak had an outstanding credit of "several hundred dollars" at the HBC outpost in Tree River from his trapping efforts. A letter from C.T. Christie to Sergeant Anderton, contained in Doak's service record, lists the exact amount as $205.91. All sources in R196-158-9-E, 1905-1921. RG 18-G, vol 3466, file 4396. LAC.

2. Letter from Stuart Wood to RCMP Commander Edmonton, January 9, 1924. RG 18, vol 3293, 1922-HQ-681-G-1, vol 2. LAC.

3. Thomas P. O'Kelly, "Western Arctic District Alleged Murder at Kent Peninsula," December 24, 1921. RG 18 vol 3289, file HQ-681-G-1. LAC.

4. Aupilaarjuk et al., *Perspectives on Traditional Law*, 164. Since Toktogan's first husband was dead — killed in Pugnana's June massacre — any member of the band could claim vengeance on his behalf.

5. O'Kelly, "Western Arctic District Alleged Murder at Kent Peninsula," December 24, 1921.

6. Testimony of Cyril Uingnek, Trial transcript, *King v Alikomiak* (re murder of Binder and Doak), July 18, 1923. RG 13, vol 1526, vol 1. LAC.

7. Ibid.

8. From the testimony of Daniel Harrison Woolams, RCMP Constable for Tree River. Trial transcript, *King v Alikomiak*, July 18. RG 13 C-1, vol 1526, "Alikomiak," vol 1, Part 1. LAC.

9. Otto Binder, folio 1919–1922. JHB/ek, March 1986. HBCA.

10. Testimony of Woolams, RCMP Constable for Tree River. Trial transcript, *King v Alikomiak*, July 18. Sylvia Van Kirk has noted that, in the company's early years, HBC men often made arrangements for their Indigenous wives and children to partner with other men when they left the country (*Many Tender Ties: Women in Fur Trade Society, 1670–1870* [Norman: University of Oklahoma Press, 1983], 15). The practice was far from universal and did not continue into the company's later years, nor did it preclude individual cases of jealousy erupting in violence. Aside from the testimony, there is no proof Binder and Cyril had entered into any understanding as to Toktogan's fate once Binder was transferred east.

11. Corporal Doak's reports, cited in the *Annual Report of the RCMP for the Year Ended September 30, 1922* (Ottawa: Thomas Mulvey, 1923), 23.

12. One often-repeated tale from the trial indicates Cyril's creative abilities as a translator. On the opening day of court, Dubuc instructed Cyril to "explain to the native that he was a judge who would decide their fate." When Cyril replied there was no word for judge in the Inuit language, Dubuc told him to find "another title." After much deliberation, Cyril settled upon "the captain of the ship." This exchange was not captured in the

official court transcript, but the possibly apocryphal tale was recounted in "World's Queerest Murder Trial," *Toronto Star Weekly*, October 27, 1923.

13. Lisa Beiler, "Alikomiak and Tatamigana: Justice and Injustice in the Canadian Arctic," MA Thesis, University of Waterloo, 2016: 167. Inuit is one of the Eskaleut language family, which contains four major languages that are further subdivided into sixteen unique dialects (Louis-Jacques Dorais, *The Language of the Inuit: Syntax, Semantics and Society in the Arctic* [Montreal: McGill-Queen's University Press, 2010], 27). "While mutual intelligibility between contiguous dialects is generally high, speakers of widely separated dialects may have great difficulty understanding each other." (David Damas [volume editor], *Handbook of North American Indians*, vol 5 [Arctic] [Washington: Smithsonian Institution, 1984], 56). Significant differences in lexicon, pronunciation, grammar, and vocabulary between dialects precluded fluent communication (Dorais, *The Language of the Inuit*, 116–127).

14. S.T. Wood, "Re: Murder of Reg. No. 4395, Corp. Doak, WA and Otto Binder by Eskimo Prisoner Alikomiak." July 21, 1922. RG vol 3293, file 1922-HQ-681-G-4. LAC.

15. Beiler argues that Cyril's "lingering animosity" toward Alikomiak impacted the way he translated at trial (170–171). She also questions whether Cyril's loyalty to the RCMP coloured his translations (171). Other researchers have argued the problem is inherent in all translators and interpreters because "all communication is dependent on his or her agenda and positions" (Richard Dauenhauer, Nora Marks Dauenhauer, "The Interpreter as Contact Point: Avoiding Collision in Tlingit America," in John Sutton-Lutz [ed.] *Myth and Memory* (Vancouver: University of British Columbia Press, 2007), 9).

16. Crime Report of J.H. Bonshor, April 8, 1922. RG 18, vol 3293, 1922-HQ-681-G-4. LAC.

17. Toktogan's statement, April 14, 1922, appended to Crime Report by J.H. Bonshor, April 8, 1922.

18. From the preamble of the "Statement of the Accused" Alikomiak, taken on April 17, 1923, "in front of Constable D.H. Woolams, Cyril Uingnek and Toktogan." RG 13 C-1, vol 1526, "Alikomiak," vol 1, Part 1. LAC.

19. Report by Stuart Wood, July 1, 1922. RG 18, vol 3293, 1922-HQ-681-G-1, vol 1. LAC.

20. Statement of Cst. Woolams for the preliminary hearing, cited in Crime Report by S.T. Wood, August 13, 1923. RG 18, vol 3293, 1922-HQ-681-G-4. LAC.

21. Statement of Ayalegak, cited in Crime Report by S.T. Wood, August 13, 1923. RG 18, vol 3293, 1922-HQ-681-G-4. LAC. See also statement by C.H. Clarke, April 15, 1922. RG 18, vol 3293, 1922-HQ-681-G-4. LAC, and S.T. Wood, "Notes Re: Murder of Cpl. W.A. Doak and Otto Binder by Eskimo Prisoner Alikomiak." Undated. RG 18, vol 3293, 1922-HQ-681-G-4. LAC.

22. Testimony of Cyril Uingnek and D.H. Woolams at the preliminary hearing, cited in Crime Report by S.T. Wood, August 13, 1923. RG vol 3293, 1922-HQ-681-G-4. LAC.

23. Statement by Cyril Uingnek, cited in the Crime Report by S.T. Wood, August 13, 1923.

24. Ibid.

25. Alikomiak's "Statement of the Accused," April 17, 1923. RG 13 C-1, vol 1526, "Alikomiak," vol 1, Part 1. LAC. See also Statement by Cyril Uingnek, cited in the Crime Report by S.T. Wood, August 13, 1923.

26. Beiler reached a similar conclusion, noting the Inuit lacked the experience or knowledge needed to reasonably predict what the RCMP or courts might do to those who commit murder (79).

27. The only exception was Alikomiak's second interrogation on June 30, 1922. This statement, taken while Alikomiak was being held in Aklavik, was interpreted by Billy Kemiksena. It contained so many contradictions and significant differences from his prior statement that Wood deemed it necessary to conduct a final interview.

28. Statement of C.H. Clarke, April 15, 1922. RG 18, vol 3293, 1922-HQ-681-G-4. LAC.

Chapter Eighteen: Closing Arguments

1. Quoted in a letter from RCMP Commissioner C. Starnes to Cory's father, NWT Commissioner W.W. Cory, October 22, 1923. RG 85, vol 607, 2580, 1923–1926. LAC.

2. Judge Dubuc closing statements. Trial transcipt, *King v Alikomiak* (murders of Binder and Doak), July 18, 1923. RG 13 C-1, vol 1526 "Alikomiak," vol 1, Part 1. LAC.

3. Quoted in Graham Price, "The King v Alikomiak," in Dale Gibson and W. Wesley Pue (eds.) *Glimpses of Canadian Legal History* (Winnipeg: Legal Research Institute of the University of Manitoba, 1991), 231.

4. Ken S. Coates and William R. Morrison, "'To Make These Tribes Understand': The Trial of Alikomiak and Tatamigana," in *Strange Things Done: Murder in Yukon History* (Montreal: McGill-Queen's University Press, 2004), 116.

5. Kenn Harper, "Taissumani, February 1, 1924: The Only Hanging of Inuit in Canada," *Nunatsiaq News*, January 27, 2006.

6. "Eskimo Pair Will Likely Be Hanged." *Hamilton Herald*, October 24, 1923.

7. Sidney L. Harring, "The Rich Men of the Country: Canadian Law in the Land of the Copper Inuit, 1914–1930," *Ottawa Law Review* 21, no. 1 (1989): 22.

8. Letter from Lucien Dubuc to the Secretary of State, September 29, 1923. RG13 C-1, vol 1, Part 1, vol 1526, CC 207, No. 24861. LAC. Rev. William D. Reeve, Anglican Bishop for Toronto, was thinking along the same lines in his letter to the Department of Justice: "May I offer a suggestion which came into my mind the other day? Imprisonment or banishment would not be adequate but what about flogging! I am inclined to think that the application of the lash would have a greater moral and deterrent effect than anything else." (Letter from Bishop W. Reeve to the Chief of Remission, Department of Justice, December 6, 1923. RG 13 C-1, vol 1526, "Alikomiak," vol 2. LAC).

9. Report from Stuart Wood to Cortlandt Starnes, July 20, 1923. RG 13, vol 271, 1519–1539, 1922. LAC.

10. Telegram from Lucien Dubuc to E.L. Newcombe, September 17, 1923. RG 13, vol 271, 1519–1539, 1922. LAC.

11. Letter from S. Wood to C. Starnes, September 1, 1923. RG 18, vol 3293, 1922-HQ-681-G-1, vol 2. LAC.

12. Letter for Lucien Dubuc to the Department of the Secretary of State, September 29, 1923. CC 207, No. 24861, RG 13, vol 1, Part 1, C-1, vol 1526. LAC.

13. Judge Dubuc's report to the Secretary of State, September 22, 1923. RG 13, vol 1526, Part 1. LAC.

Chapter Nineteen: Men of Uncertain Age

1. Letter from J.R. Lucas to the Department of Justice, September 17, 1923. RG 13 C-1, vol 1526. LAC. Lucas's letters to the editors appeared in the *Edmonton Journal* on September 14, 1923, and the *Calgary Herald* on September 15, 1923.

2. See, for example, "Canadian Law Must Replace That of Eskimo," *The Gazette*, October 24, 1923.

3. "Personal" letter from Cortlandt Starnes to M.F. Gallagher, Dept. of Justice, November 28, 1923. RG 18, vol 3293, 1922-HQ-681-G-1, vol 2. LAC.

4. "To Hang Eskimos Would Be Unjust Says Dr. Grenfell," *Toronto Daily Star*, November 21, 1923.

5. Dozens of such letters are retained in RG 13 C-1, vol 1526, vols 1 and 2. LAC; see, for example, a handwritten letter dated September 27, 1923 from C.J. Ago.

6. Letter from C. Starnes to the Minister of Justice, October 4, 1923. RG 13 C-1, vol 1526, vol 1, Part 1. LAC.

7. From an extract of the police report by S.T. Wood, July 2, 1922. RG 13 C-1, vol 1526, "Alikomiak," vol 1, Part 1. LAC.

8. "Death Sentence To Be Imposed on Two Eskimos," *Ottawa Morning Journal*, November 3, 1923.

9. "Personal" letter from C. Starnes to W.W. Cory, October 24, 1923. RG 85, vol 607, 2580, 1923–1926. LAC.

10. Letter from S.T. Wood to RCMP Edmonton Command, July 2, 1922. RG vol 3293, 1922-HQ-681-G-4. LAC.

11. Knud Rasmussen, *Intellectual Culture of the Copper Eskimo: Report of the Fifth Thule Expedition, 1921–1924,* vol 9. Copenhagen: Gyldendalske Boghandel, 1932: 279.

12. In Aupilaarjuk et al.'s *Perspectives on Traditional Law* (Iqalut: Nunavut Arctic College, 1999), 76, hunting initiation begins by age seven with the trapping of birds and small mammals, followed by a first kill of a large mammal just before boys reach their teen years. Richard Condon, in his seminal work *Inuit Youth: Growth and Change in the Canadian Arctic* (New Brunswick NJ: Rutgers University Press, 1987) concurs. David Damas (volume editor of *Handbook of North American Indians,*

vol 5 (Arctic) [Washington: Smithsonian Institution 1984], 586) notes that boys begin hunting with their fathers by age twelve.

13. Beiler, 38.

14. Aupilaarjuk et al., *Perspectives on Traditional Law*, 170.

15. Jeffrey S. Leon, "The Development of Canadian Juvenile Justice: A Background for Reform," *Osgoode Hall Law Journal* 15, no. 1 (1977): 71–106. See also the Canadian Department of Justice report "The Evolution of Juvenile Justice in Canada, 2004." The Canadian Act was based on the *Prohibitions of Offenders Act* of 1907 approved by the British Parliament, as well as England's *Children's Act* of 1908.

Chapter Twenty: Meanwhile, South of Sixty ...

1. Letter from D.M. Martin to MacKenzie King, October 9, 1923. RG 13, vol 1526, vol 1. LAC.

2. "Ask for Clemency Condemned Eskimos: At Least Seven Petitions Have Been Opened in Toronto," *Ottawa Citizen,* October 22, 1923.

3. "Peace River Election," *Manitoba Free Press*, February 28, 1906. Dubuc had campaigned in Peace River, defeating the Liberal candidate James Cornwall. When his win was vacated, Dubuc filed a lawsuit against the province demanding it recognize the election results, but he lost both the suit and his seat in the legislature ("The Peace River Case," *Manitoba Free Press*, March 20, 1906).

4. Letter from Lucien Dubuc to the Department of the Secretary of State, September 29, 1923. RG 13 C-1, vol 1526, "Alikomiak," vol 1, Part 1, CC 207, No. 24861. LAC. Dubuc prided himself on his many career "firsts," including being the first judge in Alberta to hold trials in French in 1924 (Biography of Chief Judge Lucien Dubuc, Lucien Dubuc Fonds, 1888–1979, PR 2026, Provincial Archives of Alberta).

5. Cited in Ken S. Coates and William R. Morrison, "'To Make These Tribes Understand': The Trial of Alikomiak and Tatamigana," in *Strange Things Done: Murder in Yukon History* (Montreal: McGill-Queen's University Press, 2004), 117. Those holding opposing views were in the minority but just as vocal. Missionary Eldon Merritt wrote: "Now what the Eskimo here want is an example made of some of them, and I think there will never be a better case.... It seems to me the only way to prove to them that our law is for them is to see the law enforced.

Don't you think it needs some drastic measure to stop them taking life and to protect the few whites who are in the country?" (from a letter quoted in "Re: Murder of Reg. No. 4395, Corp. Doak, WA and Otto Binder by Eskimo Prisoner Alikomiak." July 21, 1922. RG vol 3293, file 1922-HQ-681-G-4. LAC).

6. An entire section of RG 13, vol 1526, vols 1 and 2. LAC is dedicated to Dubuc's correspondence after his return to Edmonton.

7. See, for example, "The Long Arm of Justice," *Leeds Mercury*, February 4, 1924 or "Canadian Sympathy," *Liverpool Daily Post and Mercury*, February 5, 1924.

8. Letter from C. Starnes to M.F. Gallagher, November 10, 1923. RG 18, vol 3293, 1922-HQ-681-G-1, vol 2. LAC.

9. "Personal" letter from C. Starnes to H.M. Newson, October 30, 1923. RG 18, vol 3293, 1922-HQ-681-G-1, vol 2. LAC.

10. Letter from H.M. Newson to C. Starnes, November 7, 1923. RG 18, vol 3293, 1922-HQ-681-G-1, vol 2. LAC.

11. "Report Re: Arthur E. McFarlane" by Constable J.E. Robson, November 10, 1923. RG 18, vol 3293, 1922-HQ-681-G-1, vol 2. LAC.

12. Letter from H.M. Newson to C. Starnes, November 14, 1923. RG 18, vol 3293, 1922-HQ-681-G-1, vol 2. LAC.

13. Letter (G. 449.4) from Cortlandt Starnes to J. Ritchie, October 26, 1923. RG, vol 3293, 1922-HQ-681-G-1, vol 1. LAC.

14. Ibid.

15. Letter from Cortlandt Starnes to G.L. Jennings, October 23, 1923. RG 18, vol 3293, 1922-HQ-681-G-1, vol 1. LAC.

16. Telegram from J. Ritchie to C. Starnes, October 23, 1923. RG 18, vol 3293, 1922-HQ-681-G-1, vol 2. LAC.

17. Confidential Letter from Inspector Wood to Superintendent J. Ritchie RCMP Edmonton, February 10, 1924. RG 18, vol 3293, file 1922-HQ-681-G-1 vol 2. LAC.

18. Starnes issued two reports on the same day. In the first, entitled "Special Constable Gill," Starnes opened with a thinly veiled "I told you so," writing he "begs to report that he foresaw the difficulty in sending anyone … to act as hangman at Herschel Island" (C. Starnes to M.F. Gallagher, October 31, 1923. RG 18, vol 3293, 1922-HQ-681-G-1, vol 2. LAC). That Starnes had been complicit in the scheme all along

was conveniently forgotten. Starnes tackled the "digging of the graves for condemned Eskimos" under separate cover (C. Starnes to M.F. Gallagher, October 31, 1923. RG 18, vol 3293, 1922-HQ-681-G-1, vol 2. LAC).

19. Letter from C. Starnes to M.F. Gallagher, October 31, 1923. RG 18, vol 3293, 1922-HQ-681-G-1, vol 2. LAC.

20. Ibid.

21. "Death Sentence To Be Imposed on Two Eskimos," *Ottawa Morning Journal*, November 3, 1923.

22. Letter from W. R. Lindsay to C. Starnes, May 31, 1923. See also letter from L.B. Caulkill to G.L. Jennings, March 24, 1925, both in R196-158-9-E, 1905–1921. RG 18-G, vol 3466, file 4396. LAC.

23. Memorandum from Inspector Lindsay to Starnes, May 31, 1923. William Doak's Service Records, R196-158-9-E, 1905–1921. RG 18-G, vol 3466, file 4396. LAC. According to a memorandum included in Doak's service file the headstone's maker was not paid until September 27, 1927.

24. Letter from L.W. Doak to RCMP, April 19, 1923. William Doak's Service Records, R196-158-9-E, 1905–1921. RG 18-G, vol 3466, file 4396. LAC. Aside from the honour such an interment conveyed, the family wanted Bill's grave to be in a more accessible area so that they might visit.

25. Report by J.H. Bonshor, October 15, 1923, William Doak's Service Records, R196-158-9-E, 1905–1921. RG 18-G, vol 3466, file 4396. LAC.

26. Confidential Letter from Inspector Wood to Superintendent J. Ritchie of the RCMP Edmonton detachment, February 10, 1924, RG18, vol 3293, file 1922-HQ-681-G-1, vol 2. LAC.

27. Letter from C. Starnes to W.W. Cory, October 24, 1923, RG 85, vol 607, 2580, 1923–1926. LAC, referencing a prior letter from Cory stating, "I am glad that you are taking the view that the Eskimos are the wards of the Commissioner of the North West Territories. This has always been our contention." Lisa Beiler reached the same conclusion in her 2016 MA thesis, arguing that Inuit, as residents of the NWT, fell under the jurisdiction of the Department of the Interior (117).

28. Constance Backhouse, *Colour-Coded: A Legal History of Racism in Canada* (Toronto: University of Toronto Press, 1999), 1–18. See also Beiler, 117.

Chapter Twenty-One: Stunt Man

1. A photograph of the 1921 judicial party shows a proud Thorne in full uniform towering over the rest of the court officers. July, 1921. Lucien Dubuc Fonds, Provincial Archives of Alberta, A3663.

2. Telegram sent by C. Starnes to Vancouver RCMP Commander October 8, 1923. RG 18, vol 3293, 1922-HQ-681-G-1, vol 1. LAC.

3. "One Policeman to Carry Sentence of Death to the Arctic," *Sault Daily Star*, October 20, 1923.

4. Starnes stated as much in a letter to Vancouver Commander, demanding acknowledgement of his October 8 telegram as it was "his authority to proceed with the executions" (Letter from C. Starnes to Vancouver RCMP Commander, October 20, 1923. D.487 L.1, RG 18, vol 3293, 1922-HQ-681-G-1, vol 1. LAC).

5. Letter from T.A. Wroughton to C. Starnes, October 9, 1923. RG 18, vol 3293, 1922-HQ-681-G-1, vol 1. LAC.

6. Report by H.G. Thorne, March 31, 1924. RG 18, vol 3293, 1922-HQ-681-G-1, vol 2. LAC. Thorne left Edmonton by CN Rail on October 5, arriving in Vancouver on October 7, 1923. Thorne would eventually return from Herschel on February 19, arriving in Vancouver on March 31, 1924.

7. Telegram from Sgt. Thorne to C. Starnes, October 26, 1923. RG 18, vol 3293, 1922-HQ-681-G-1, vol 1. LAC.

8. As noted in a letter from C. Starnes to M.F. Gallagher, November 19, 1923. RG 18, vol 3293, 1922-HQ-681-G-1, vol 2. LAC.

9. Letter from C. Starnes to M.F. Gallagher, November 15, 1923. RG 18, vol 3293, 1922-HQ-681-G-1, vol 2. LAC.

10. Telegram from C. Starnes to H.G. Thorne, November 19, 1923. RG 18, vol 3293, 1922-HQ-681-G-1, vol 2. LAC

11. Sgt. Thorne "Report of Patrol from Edmonton to Herschel Island and Return." March 31, 1924. RG 18-vol 3293, file 1922-HQ-681-G-1, vol 2. LAC.

12. Letter from Stuart Wood to. Cortlandt Starnes, September 1, 1923. RG 18, vol 3293, 1922-HQ-681-G-1, vol 2. LAC.

13. The *News of the World* report was reprinted verbatim in the *Edmonton Bulletin* ("A Hot Arctic Story," January 17, 1924).

Chapter Twenty-Two: The Eternal Hunting Grounds

1. From Knud Rasmussen's journals, cited in Kenn Harper, "More on the Herschel Island Hangings," *Nunatsiaq News*, February 3, 2006.

2. Stuart Wood, Crime Report Re: Alikomiak — murder of Cpt. WA Doak and Otto Binder, February 2, 1924. RG 18 vol 3293, vol 2. LAC.

3. Kenn Harper, "Taissumani, February 1, 1924: The Only Hanging of Inuit in Canada," *Nunatsiaq News*, January 27, 2006.

4. From a report by Knud Rasmussen, cited in Coates and Morrison's "'To Make These Tribes Understand,'" in *Strange Things Done: Murder in Yukon History* (Montreal: McGill-Queen's University Press, 2004), 119.

5. Kenn Harper, "Taissumani, February 1, 1924: The Only Hanging of Inuit in Canada," *Nunatsiaq News*, January 27, 2006.

6. Stuart Wood, Crime Report, February 2, 1924. RG 18, vol 3293, file 1922-HQ-681-G-1, vol 2. LAC.

7. Cpl J.P. Pennefather, "Schedule of Jurymen," RG 85, vol 607, 2580, 1923–1926. LAC.

8. Stuart Wood, Crime Report, February 2, 1924. RG 18, vol 3293, file 1922-HQ-681-G-1, vol 2. LAC.

9. A.A. Carroll as the source of the rumour comes from Philip H. Godsell, *Arctic Trader: The Account of Twenty Years with the Hudson's Bay Company,* (Toronto: MacMillan, 1946), 296. At least two newspapers — the *Ottawa Citizen* ("Herschel Island Eskimos Executed," March 8, 1924) and the *Toronto Star* ("Eskimos in Scaffold Blamed Mounted Police," March 9, 1924) cite Sergeant Thorne as the source of Alikomiak's final words. According to Thorne, Alikomiak "declared that the police had long been the enemies of their people" (from the *Ottawa Citizen* report.) Still another report in the *Ottawa Citizen* ("Declares Eskimos Prepared to Die," May 5, 1924) attributed different final words to the doomed Inuit, claiming the men said "that they deserved their fate and were prepared to die for their crimes."

10. Harper, "Taissumani, February 1, 1924: The Only Hanging of Inuit in Canada."

11. Form 71 (section 1068) — the autopsy report for Tatamigana, certified by P.E. Doyle, Assistant Surgeon RCMP. RG 13 C-1, vol 1526, "Alikomiak," vol 1, Part 1. LAC.

12. "Information of the Witness — Alikomiak," February 1, 1924. RG 85, vol 607, 2580, 1923–1926. LAC.

13. Wood. Crime Report: Tatamigana Execution, February 2, 1924. RG 18, vol 3293, file 1922-HQ-681-G-1, vol 2. LAC. A virtually identical report was created on the same day for Alikomiak, with the exact same closing line.

14. Quoted in a telegram from RCMP Command Edmonton to Cortlandt Starnes, March 8, 1924. RG 18, vol 3293, 1922-HQ-681-G-1, vol 2. LAC.

15. "Hangman Is Annoyed by Amateur Execution," *Globe and Mail*, February 27, 1924.

16. "Execution of Two Eskimos a Costly Matter to Canada," *Ottawa Citizen*, May 9, 1925.

17. Knud Rasmussen, *Across Arctic America: Narrative of the Fifth Thule Expedition* (New York: G.P. Putnam's Sons, 1927), 280.

18. Letter from E.L. Newcombe to Cortlandt Starnes, November 19, 1922.

19. Coates and Morrison, "'To Make These Tribes Understand,'" 119. Legal scholar Sidney Harring dismissed the Herschel court as "a staged trial that was *perhaps* procedurally correct but undoubtedly unjust." Sidney L. Harring, "The Rich Men of the Country: Canadian Law in the Land of the Copper Inuit, 1914–1930," *Ottawa Law Review* 21, no. 4 (1989) (emphasis added). Harring hedged his assessment because he drew all knowledge of the crime and trials from newspaper reports (13).

20. Harring, 26.

21. See, for example, Shelagh D. Grant, *Arctic Justice: On Trial for Murder Pond Inlet, 1923* (Montreal: McGill-Queen's University Press, 2002), 244.

22. Knud Rasmussen, *Intellectual Culture of the Copper Eskimo: Report of the Fifth Thule Expedition, 1921–1924,* vol 9 (Copenhagen: Gyldendalske Boghandel, 1932), 64.

23. Indigenous and Northern Affairs Canada, "Nunavut — September 2003," www.aadnc-aandc.gc.ca, accessed November 1, 2017.

24. *A Circumpolar Inuit Declaration of Sovereignty in the Arctic*, www.inuit-circumpolar.ca, accessed November 1, 2017.

25. Rasmussen does not specify whether it was Alikomiak's father or Tatamigana's. He says only that "one of the two men had an old father

living on Kent Peninsula." Rasmussen, *Intellectual Culture of the Copper Eskimo*, 63. Philip Godsell suggests a far less romantic version of the story, in which the father's shame over his son's crime prompted the suicide (*Arctic Trader: The Account of Twenty Years with the Hudson's Bay Company* [Toronto: MacMillan, 1946], 295).

26. Account by Knud Rasmussen, cited in Kenn Harper, "Taissumani: More on the Herschel Island Hangings," *Nunatsiaq News*, February 3, 2006. Rasmussen also described the incident in less detail in *Across Arctic America: Narrative of the Fifth Thule Expedition* (New York: G.P. Putnam's Sons, 1927), 280.

27. Harper, "Taissumani, February 1, 1924: The Only Hanging of Inuit in Canada."

Image Credits

11   Image by author.

24   *St. John Daily Telegraph*, July 26, 1922.

27   Lucien Dubuc Fonds, Provincial Archives of Alberta, A3705.

29   LAC, Image PA-102577.

32   LAC, R196-174-7-E, 1916.

35   George Wilkins, 1917.

36   LAC, Alikomiak (Eskimo), Department of Justice, G 13 vol 1 Pt 1 1526.

39   LAC, Alikomiak (Eskimo), Department of Justice, RG 13 vol 1 Pt 1 1526.

47   Lucien Dubuc Fonds, Provincial Archives of Alberta, A3687.

49   Lucien Dubuc Fonds, Provincial Archives of Alberta, A3659.

50   Lucien Dubuc Fonds, Provincial Archives of Alberta, A3719.

58   LAC, Image 3213533.

62   Glenbow Museum, PA-3946-56-8.

67   Yukon Archives, Anglican Church of Canada, Diocese of Yukon Fonds, 86/61, #24.

72   Knud Rasmussen, 1927.

77   Detail of LAC, PA-019353.

78   Miriam Green Ellis. University of Alberta, Bruce Peel Special Collections, Image 291.

Index

A MATTER OF CONSCIENCE
JAMES BARTLEMAN

A novel of love and betrayal dealing with the biggest issues facing Canada's Indigenous Peoples today.

In the summer of 1972, a float plane carrying a team of child welfare officials lands on a river flowing through the Yellow Dog Indian Reserve. Their mission is to seize the twin babies of an Indigenous couple as part of an illegal scheme cooked up by the federal government to adopt out tens of thousands of Indigenous children to white families. The baby girl, Brenda, is adopted and raised by a white family in Orillia.

Meanwhile, that same summer, a baby boy named Greg is born to a white middle-class family. At the age of eighteen, Greg leaves home for the first time to earn money to help pay for his university expenses. He drinks heavily and becomes embroiled in the murder of a female student from a residential school.

The destinies of Brenda and Greg intersect in this novel of passion, confronting the murder and disappearance of Indigenous women and the infamous Sixties Scoop.

DROP DEAD
A Horrible History of Hanging in Canada
LORNA POPLAK

**Governments all over the world are consistently outpaced
by digital change, and are falling behind.**

Take a journey through notable cases in Canada's criminal justice history, featuring well-known and some less-well-known figures from the past. You'll meet Arthur Ellis, Canada's most famous hangman, whose work outfit was a frock coat and striped trousers, often with a flower pinned to his lapel. And you will also encounter other memorable characters, including the man who was hanged twice and the gun-toting bootlegger who was the only woman ever executed in Alberta.

Drop Dead: A Horrible History of Hanging in Canada illustrates how trial, sentencing, and punishment operated in Canada's first century, and examines the relevance of capital punishment today. Along the way, learn about the mathematics and physics behind hangings, as well as disturbing facts about bungled executions and wrongful convictions.

DR. ORONHYATEKHA
Security, Justice, and Equality
MICHELLE A. HAMILTON AND KEITH
JAMIESON

2016 Ontario Historical Society Joseph Brant Award — Winner 2017
Speaker's Book Award — Shortlisted

A man of two cultures in an era where his only choices
were to be a trailblazer or get left by the wayside.

Dr. Oronhyatekha ("Burning Sky"), born in the Mohawk nation on the Six Nations of the Grand River territory in 1841, led an extraordinary life, rising to prominence in medicine, sports, politics, fraternalism, and business. He was one of the first Indigenous physicians in Canada, the first to attend Oxford University, a Grand River representative to the Prince of Wales during the 1860 royal tour, a Wimbledon rifle champion, the chairman of the Grand General Indian Council of Ontario, and Grand Templar of the International Order of Good Templars. He counted among his friends some of the most powerful people of the day, including John A. Macdonald and Theodore Roosevelt. He successfully challenged the racial criteria of the Independent Order of Foresters to become its first non-white member and ultimately its supreme chief ranger.

At a time when First Nations Peoples struggled under assimilative government policy and society's racial assumptions, his achievements were remarkable.

Oronhyatekha was raised among a people who espoused security, justice, and equality as their creed. He was also raised in a Victorian society guided by God, honour, and duty. He successfully interwove these messages throughout his life, and lived as a man of significant accomplishments in both worlds.

Book Credits

Acquiring Editor: Scott Fraser
Developmental Editor: Dominic Farrell
Project Editor: Elena Radic
Copy Editor: Heather Bean
Proofreader: Dawn Hunter

Cover Designer: Laura Boyle
Interior Designer: Sophie Paas-Lang

Publicist: Elham Ali

Dundurn

Publisher: J. Kirk Howard
Vice-President: Carl A. Brand
Editorial Director: Kathryn Lane
Artistic Director: Laura Boyle
Production Manager: Rudi Garcia
Manager, Accounting and Technical Services: Livio Copetti

Editorial: Allison Hirst, Dominic Farrell, Jenny McWha, Rachel Spence,
Elena Radic, Melissa Kawaguchi
Marketing and Publicity: Kendra Martin, Elham Ali, Heather McLeod
Design and Production: Sophie Paas-Lang

dundurn.com   dundurnpress
@dundurnpress   dundurnpress
dundurnpress   info@dundurn.com

FIND US ON NETGALLEY & GOODREADS TOO!

DUNDURN